MAXIMUM
CAPACITY

Encouraging Living Life to the Fullest Every Day!

Jamila K. Brown

Illustrations by
Sarah Griffith

Library of Congress Control Number: 2022912407
ISBN: 9798839271968
Book Cover design by Jamila Kamaria Brown.
Interior drawings by Sarah Griffith.
Published by: Jamila Kamaria Brown

That we will not forget how great we are as women,
that we will remember that we are daughters of the King,
and because of His great love we have hope!
Encouraging women to go on, press on, and keep on,
even in the midst of life's troubles, worries, and issues.
Encouraging that abundant life!
With God, you are enough, and that enough is worth
sharing with the world.
No more holding back, it's time to shine.
No more playing small.

"I have come that they might have life, and that they
may have it more abundantly."
John 10:10b NKJV

TABLE OF CONTENTS

LET'S HAVE SOME FUN! ENCOURAGE YOUR GROUP IN DIFFERENT WAYS...

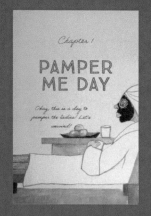
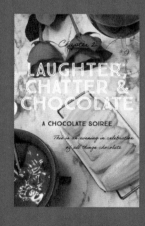
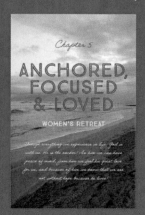

ENCOURAGE THEM TO SPEND TIME WITH THEIR SISTAS, BESTIES, AND FRIENDS

98

118

ENCOURAGE THEM TO ENCOURAGE ANOTHER

ENCOURAGE THEM TO HONOR WHO CAME BEFORE & BUILD THEIR OWN LEGACY

126

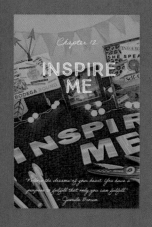

INTRODUCTION

Event planning or activity planning in its essence involves collaboration, working with groups of people, engaging your audience, and providing something of value. At the end, we just want to know that it was worth it. Worth the hours put in behind the scenes to ensure the "day of" comes out just as planned. Why is this even more important now, right now, at this moment in history? With everything going on around us, it's easy to get lost in the chaos, the fear, the anticipation of what's next. Finding ways to stay in the moment, this moment, enjoying the good things in life; finding ways to ground yourself to remember that we will get through this; reflecting on your values, things you enjoy, and the people you share your life with, can help take your focus off all the negativity, worry, concern and uncertainty. Focusing on these things, has been shown throughout history to lead to increased stress, anxiety, health concerns, and will ultimately leave us living beyond our maximum capacity. How do we bring it back to taking things one day at a time? How do we enjoy the things in life that we once did? How do we get to a new place of normalcy with the chaos of life surrounding us? Planning for a new environment where health and hygiene are super important. Planning for a new crowd where uncertainty fills the room first. We are planning to help provide those attending with something of value that they can take with them in the days ahead to encourage them. Encouraging them to take time to listen to themselves, their feelings, their hopes, their dreams, their concerns, and let go of the things they cannot change. Finding ways to create a space where we are no longer just running at maximum capacity, but we are learning to take each day as it comes. Making that day beautiful, finding value in that day, learning something that can help them in the days ahead. Reminding them of the treasure they are. Living life encouraged. We are creating moments, helping to realize dreams, and we are constantly thinking outside of the box. Creativity is our language. We are helping others step away from the humdrum of it all, even if just for an hour or so to enjoy living life to the fullest. We are the administrators, creators, coordinators, facilitators, moderators, managers and party planners. My hope is that this book will help both you and your group live life a little closer to your fullest potential. As you plan your next event, remember,

"It's all in the details."

- Author unknown

PLANNER
CARE IDEAS

Taking a few minutes to care for the party planner.

PLANNER CARE

Sometimes we live our lives full to the brim, running from one day or event to the next with a checklist full of items that all demand our attention. In a business that is totally customer driven, the planner can sometimes get lost in the hustle. I must admit, I am not exempt. Burnout is no joke and can be taxing to our bodies, mind and overall wellbeing. Through the years, I'm learning the necessity of a work-life balance and the importance of taking time to care for myself, even if just for a few minutes here or there.

This is your reminder that it is essential to take care of the event planner, that's you! As you plan your group's next event or night out, utilize the Planner Care Tips that are sprinkled throughout this book or be encouraged to think of a few of your own. All of these Planner Care Tips are also listed in this section for you.

Take some time to plan for yourself, plan for your needs, and to say no if needed. Sometimes before show time, it is necessary to stop for a few minutes to refocus and take a break to care for yourself. You're not ready for the lights and you're not ready for that camera just yet.

Be encouraged to take care of your needs and be attentive to your own wellbeing so that you can party on!

Spending a day on the beach, enjoying your favorite ice cream cone, meeting up with a friend for lunch, taking a quick walk or investing a few minutes to update your vision board, may be just what you need to replenish yourself.

The work will always be there, your health may not. Write out one thing you can do this week to improve your work-life balance here:

CHAPTER 1

Okay! So you have planned out your Pamper Me Day, you've sent out your invites, purchased a few things and snacks, and now you are ready to party! 30 minutes to an hour before your party, take a few minutes to:

- Freshen up
- Take a breath
- Pray
- Sit down for a minute
- Reflect on the fact that as a leader you need to replenish, rejuvenate, and step away for a while every now and then. It's difficult to take care of others if you are not taking care of yourself. Set a date to do something that you enjoy.

DATE _____

PUT ON YOUR FLIP FLOPS AND GET READY TO PARTY!

Find a workout that you can do at least 3-4 days a week. Write out your plan for the week here:

SUNDAY _____

MONDAY _____

TUESDAY _____

WEDNESDAY _____

THURSDAY _____

FRIDAY _____

SATURDAY _____

CHAPTER 2

Okay! So you have planned out your Chocolate Soiree, you've sent out your invites, set up your chocolate fountain and treats, and now you are ready to party! 30 minutes to an hour before your party, take a few minutes to:

- Freshen up

- Take a breath

- Sit down for a minute

- Step Away Moments: It is easy to get burned out, even with a great team. It can take a lot out of you emotionally, mentally and spiritually to lead other women. Think of some ways to "step away" every now and then, even if just to pray for yourself and your group. You could use some of the ideas from the Girl's Day or Night Out activities in Chapter 4 to get you started.

Find someone who can keep you lifted up in prayer. List their name here and reach out to them this week

DIP A TREAT IN CHOCOLATE, ENJOY IT, AND GET READY TO PARTY!

DRAW YOUR IDEAS HERE

LIGHTS,
CAMERA, WAIT...
OK, I'M READY
TO SHINE.
- JAMILA K. BROWN

CHAPTER 3

Okay! So you have planned out your Themed Talk, you've sent out your invites, purchased a few snacks, and now you're ready to party! 30 minutes to an hour before your party, take a few minutes to:

- Freshen up
- Take a breath
- Pray: Write out a quick prayer for yourself
- Stretch
- Sit down for a minute
- Enjoy a cold or warm beverage depending on the season and get ready to party!

PERSONAL THEME

You have a word and food item set for today, now it's time to choose a word that will describe your own goals and your vision for this year. I've found that choosing a word helps to set a direction for your year that can help you move closer to your goals. Some examples of some words I've used in the past include: Encouraged, Grateful, Courageous, Determined, and Inspired. A few other words you might use are: Focused, Appreciative, Powerful, Fearless, and Driven. Use your word to help create focus and define it so you know what you are trying to accomplish. Think about how this word will help you accomplish this task or how this word will help motivate you to reach this goal. How will this word fit into your story? For example

Theme word = Fearless

SOME QUESTIONS TO ASK YOURSELF

1. What goals have you delayed due to a fear of failure, lack of resources, or some other factor?

2. What steps would you take to reach these goals if nothing was holding you back? You may need to do some research here to determine what is needed to get from point A to point B.

3. Who can help you accomplish your goals? This can be someone already working in the field that you want to work in, a mentor or an online resource or expert that can help you take steps towards your goals.

4. How can you set goals including your date of completion to represent your word, and what action items can you write down today?

5. At the end of the year, what results would make you feel that you have lived your fearless year? Start working towards it!

6. Create a few planner spreads that incorporate your theme word in your planner throughout the year as a reminder of what you are working towards.

MY THEME
OF THE
YEAR

Fill these pages with pictures, words,
cutouts, and colors to represent your theme
for the year.

Inspire. Dream. Laugh. Live. Abundantly.

CHAPTER 4

Okay! So you have planned your Girl's Day or Night Out and you are ready to venture out on the town! 30 minutes to an hour before your day or night out, take a few minutes to:

- Sit down for a minute
- Review the directions to the outing destination
- Be encouraged: Sometimes as leaders we want everyone to get involved. Through the years I've learned that some members come and go, some stay, and some come once and never come back. Be encouraged that whoever is there is meant to be there. Focus on encouraging those that do come. Write out one way to encourage yourself here and work on that this month (check out Chapter 14 for some ideas).

I WILL ENCOURAGE MYSELF BY:

GRAB YOUR CAMERA OR CAMERA PHONE AND LET'S HAVE FUN!

3 WAYS TO TAKE ACTION ON IT THIS MONTH:

01

02

03

CHAPTER 5

Okay! So you have planned out your retreat, everyone has signed up, they are excited to go and will soon be arriving; you've packed the trunk or van with the supplies you are bringing. 30 minutes to an hour before everyone starts arriving on the first morning of the retreat, take a few minutes to:

- Freshen up
- Take a breath
- Pray over those that are attending the retreat that they will take away what they need and that you will as well
- Sit down for a minute

WRITE OUT WHY THIS RETREAT MATTERS TO YOU, AND WHAT ENCOURAGES YOU TO DO IT

JOT DOWN A FEW THINGS THAT YOU WANT TO TAKE AWAY FROM THE RETREAT HERE:

CHAPTER 6

Okay! So you have planned out your brunch, you've sent out your invites, purchased a few snacks and decorated! 30 minutes to an hour before your party, take a few minutes to:

- Freshen up
- Take a breath
- Pray
- Sit down for a minute

ENJOY A COLD BEVERAGE AND LET'S DO BRUNCH!

WRITE OUT YOUR GOALS FOR THIS EVENT AND WHAT KIND OF IMPACT YOU WANT THIS EVENT TO HAVE ON YOUR GROUP HERE:

CHAPTER 8

Okay! So you have planned out your bonfire, you've sent out your invites, and have mapped out safe places to build a bonfire. Through the years I have found that it is hard to look out for others when you are not taking care of yourself first. I have found that a great way to de-stress from day-to-day is to use your creative side. Take a few minutes to color one of the coloring sheets in Appendix C.

- Dream Chaser
- Life to the Fullest
- Inspired

CHAPTER 11

Okay! So you have planned out your workshop, you've sent out your invites, decorated the venue and you are waiting for everyone to arrive. 30 minutes to an hour before your start time, take a few minutes to:

- Freshen up
- Take a breath
- Pray
- Sit down for a minute
- Think of a few things that make you uniquely you and how these things have helped you grow as a leader. Keep these in mind as you encourage everyone that attends today's event. After all, you are a gem as well!
- **Write them out here:**

CHAPTER 12

Okay! So you have planned out your Vision Board & Goals Pop-up, you've sent out your invites, decorated the venue and you are waiting for everyone to arrive. 30 minutes to an hour before your start time, take a few minutes to:

- Freshen up

- Take a breath

- Pray

- Sit down for a minute

- Think of how you are sharing your gifts with the world. Are you living up to your full potential? Think of one or two ways to step out and follow your dreams. Let go of the fear, discouragement or doubt. God placed that dream in your heart for a reason; it is yours so step out and live it.

WRITE THEM OUT HERE:

**CREATE A VISION BOARD FOR
YOUR YEAR HERE:**

CHAPTER 13

Okay! So you have planned out your celebration, you've put together your holiday platter, decorated the venue and you are waiting for everyone to arrive. 30 minutes to an hour before your start time, take a few minutes to:

- Freshen up
- Take a breath
- Pray
- Sit down for a minute
- Reflect on the past year: What were some of the goals you wanted to accomplish with your group? Who joined and what have they added to the group? What have you learned from everyone and from yourself? What will you take from this year and how will you use what you have learned going forward?

**WRITE OUT YOUR ANSWERS
HERE:**

PLANNING FOR THE YEAR

A few things to keep in mind from the start...

PLANNING FOR THE YEAR AHEAD

DEVELOPING YOUR TEAM

Everyone brings different strengths to the overall team. Use these questions to see where everyone could thrive on your team.

1. I'd rather be doing this on my day off:

2. I've always wanted to:

3. One thing you wouldn't know just by looking at me:

4. I feel loved when:

5. This encourages me:

6. I joined the team because:

7. One thing I would like to learn is:

8. I would love to see our team:

PLANNING SESSIONS

It is important to gather your planning team occasionally to make sure that you are all on the same page in regards to your upcoming events. As a group, plan out some goals that you would like to accomplish for the year. Your activities and events can revolve around this theme. For example, the theme of this book is Encouragement, so the events and activities are geared towards encouraging in some way.

Throughout the year mini planning sessions are helpful to walk through the details of the event. For example: Who will bring what, who is responsible for this part, who is coordinating the marketing of the event, etc. Your meetings can take whatever format works for your group. You can choose one below or combine a few as needed. Have an agenda ready to go and keep track of the meeting minutes for any follow-up items and your records.

HERE ARE A FEW MEETING FORMAT EXAMPLES:

1. **Top of the month:** Meet once a month for an overall planning session to work on event or activity details, send invites, coordinate sign-up, and to get the word out.

2. **Every few weeks:** Meet every few weeks to plan certain aspects of your event. This is helpful for larger events like a retreat or workshop. You can break the retreat or workshop down into smaller parts like finding a speaker, designing marketing, coordinating food, or putting materials together for the event.

3. **Beginning and end of the year:** Set a date to plan the group's activities for the upcoming year. Invite your group to suggest ideas for activities that they would like to do. Bring your calendars and schedule out the tentative dates. If you are a part of a larger group be sure to check the overall calendar to ensure that there are no conflicting dates.

4. **As needed:** Set up planning meetings. Some events will not take as long to plan out, such as a Girl's Night Out. You just pick the location, set your time, and get the word out to your group.

SOME THINGS TO THINK ABOUT WHEN PLANNING YOUR EVENT

During the planning stages, consider these things that can impact your event's success.

1. **Consider the type of event that you want to do:**

   ○ Choose your events for the year.

   ○ Figure out the event details:

   ▶ These can include things like: choosing a date, deciding the event time, determining who will be invited & how you will invite them, setting a few event goals, and determining the event logistics. Create a checklist of what needs to be done and who will do what.

2. **Determine your overall event budget:**

   ○ Determine how much you have to spend and stay within that number! Expenses can add up fast so knowing how much you have to work with is important.

   ○ Some of the items that you may want to include in your budget depending on the type and scale of your event are:

   ▶ Venue expenses: Some may require a deposit, and some venues are cheaper midweek vs. on the weekend. Decide what you can spend on the venue if needed. The location you choose is step one in planning for the success of your event, so allocate a good amount of your budget for these expenses.

   ▶ Food & Catering: Will the food be catered or done potluck style?

   ▶ Music & Entertainment: Will you need a DJ or band, or can you use an internet music streaming site?

   ▶ Floral & Decorations: Will your venue need some sprucing up, or will a few streamers and balloons suffice?

   ▶ Activities: What items will be needed for everyone to participate in the planned activities?

   ▶ Gifts/Prizes: Are any take home gifts or prizes needed for the activities?

   ▶ Marketing/Printing: This can include fliers, tickets, invites and/or handouts. Marketing through social media can help to cut down on costs in this area.

- ▶ Rentals: Will you need to rent any tablecloths, chairs, tables, or other items?

○ For the larger items like the venue, food & catering, music & entertainment, you can request quotes from vendors and compare them for the most affordable option for your budget.

3. **If you are a part of a larger organization, does your event fit into the overall calendar?**

○ Do you need to move any events on your calendar around to make sure the majority of the group can attend?

○ Determine how much advance notice you need to give your group. For example, a workshop or retreat would need more advanced planning than a Girl's Night Out.

4. **For virtual events:**

○ Ensure your internet connectivity is good. This can be enhanced with a hotspot.

○ Sign in early to get everything set up.

○ Enable the waiting room for attendees who like to sign in early.

○ Encourage the group to turn their cameras on.

○ Smile.

○ Get help moderating the event:

- ▶ Checking in/letting attendees in
- ▶ Chatroom/Breakout room moderating
- ▶ Presenting

5. **Keep in mind that no one wants to spend every free moment attending events.**

○ Try to spread your events throughout the year. Put together a calendar for the group so they know what events are coming well in advance. This book can be used as a guide to plan a year's worth of events for your group, which are perfect for small friend groups or church groups.

6. **Enjoy the planning process.**

   ○ Remember that these events are opportunities to find inspiration, encourage those in your group, and step away every once in a while from the normal hustle. Have some fun and always remember your why - write it out if you have to.

4 WAYS TO GROW AS A PLANNER

Some ways to grow as a planner include:

1. **Take time to plan and prepare:**

   ○ Prior to each event, review your to-do items, delegate, and work with your team to get things moving.

   ○ Get to know your team, they are with you out on the front line. Know your team's strengths, weaknesses, and areas to improve.

   ○ After each event, do a quick assessment to see if you met your event goals. You can use the "After the Event Checklist" at the end of this Planning for the Year Chapter.

2. **Utilize planning tools:**

   ○ Planning tools such as this book, existing project management software, or creating your own tools can help to get the items on your list completed. I have found collaboration tools like Trello that organize your projects into boards in one glance helpful to manage large projects with multiple team members and action items.

   ○ If one of your team members is good at organizing, utilize their skills to create an overall plan of action. If someone is great at photography, use their skills to take photos at events that can be used to create marketing for future events. Everyone brings something to the table.

3. **Be inspired:**

   ○ Inspiration is all around you! Always look for ways to improve, grow, or do things better than the last time. Many professional organizations, and others in your field, have blogs that you can follow to learn and grow.

   ○ The internet is a great place to find daily inspiration ideas.

   ○ Realize that great ideas are truly not out of your reach. We all bring great ideas to the table; however, many never make it past the chopping block simply because no one knows how to make them happen. Put together a proposal for your idea(s) and bring it to your group. Someone else may know how to get your idea off the chopping block and into a realistic action item for the year.

   ○ Find something that you enjoy within your field and be great at it. Finding your niche is key to finding fulfillment. You may have always wanted to learn how to create a marketing plan, or learn some new ways to grow engagement.

4. **Create a vision for your group:**

   ○ One of the top ways to grow as a planner includes creating a shared vision for your group. Without a shared vision, you can end up with many great ideas but no goals for these ideas to work towards. No target, no direction, no collaboration.

   ○ When creating this book, my vision was: To create a fun book of activities for women's groups for the novice event planner that would not only encourage the attendees, but also be a resource to help planners grow as leaders, to grow professionally, and to stay encouraged as they are encouraging their group. I've read hundreds of articles and books on event planning, but very few if any focused on the planner's needs. To accomplish this vision, I included planner care tips, spotlights, as well as many other tips throughout the book to not just focus on the attendees but to also focus on the needs of the planner.

○ A few questions to consider when creating your vision:

► What is the purpose for your group?
► What do you want to accomplish with your activities?
► Who will your group include?
► What will define success?
► Where do you see your group in one year? Five years? Ten years?
► What do you want those who attend to take away?
► What can you accomplish today?

WE NEED ENCOURAGEMENT TOO...

In leadership sometimes we forget our team needs encouragement too. As a team we spend a lot of time developing others, building up others, and encouraging others, while our own well is sometimes running dry. Try some of the ideas below to encourage the team.

1. Call your fellow team members to see how their week was

2. Send a note or card of encouragement

3. Pray for your team - Have a prayer day/call or team up with prayer partners

4. Host a leadership team Secret Sister over the course of a few months or for the year to be revealed at the end of the year. Each member would send encouraging words, a note, a small gift or whatever would be an encouragement to her Secret Sister without revealing who she is. Everyone could do a short survey at the beginning with their favorite color, candy, activity, etc.

5. Have a mini team retreat online

6. Give thanks to the team at the next event or overall group meeting and give them flowers

7. Highlight/Spotlight a team member in your group newsletter or on the group webpage

8. Bake them some treats

9. Create SWAG items just for the leadership team. This could be a team t-shirt, tote bag, backpack, bracelet, etc.

10. Tell someone how great your team is

11. Take a leadership team photo or selfie and have it framed

FINDING WAYS TO STAY CONNECTED WITH YOUR GROUP

With everything going on, sometimes we can feel disconnected. Here are a few ways to intentionally stay connected.

1. Assign each team member a few ladies to call at least once a month. Swap groups quarterly.

2. Use an online platform for a themed group meeting or check-in every now and then.

3. Compile a list of things everyone is thankful for and send out to the group.

4. Send an encouraging word, poem, or post out to the team.

5. Redefine your group's goals.

6. Find out from each member how the group can encourage them during this time and put a few suggestions into action each month.

7. Share or have everyone post photos from past events on a shared site like a Kudoboard.

8. Have everyone sign up for a Secret Sister.

9. Meet up somewhere outdoors for a walk.

10. Take a poll for things to do.

11. Swap favorite recipes, tips on ways to move or stretch, relaxation tips, scriptures, books you're reading etc.

12. Share a favorite song or compile a group favorite's playlist.

13. Start online meetings/live events with an icebreaker.

14. Reach out by phone to those who aren't as internet savvy. Most online platforms allow attendees the option to just call in as well.

THE VENUE LAYOUT IS ONLY A PIECE OF THE PLAN. CONNECTING THE DOTS ALONG THE WAY IS WHAT MAKES AN EVENT A SUCCESS.
- JAMILA K. BROWN

SOME IDEAS TO BREAK THE ICE...

Icebreakers are great to help get conversation started at the beginning of your event. Choose one or two below for the group and have some fun!

1. Share your favorite "cheat food."

2. If you could travel anywhere, where would it be and why?

3. Share one thing you absolutely love and why.

4. What is your favorite childhood ice cream memory?

5. Share one goal you would like to accomplish before the end of the year.

6. Who is your favorite Bible woman character and why? Do you feel as if you can relate to her?

7. What is your must have summer item & why?

8. What is your favorite scripture and why?

9. Are you a night owl or early morning riser?

10. Write down a fact that no one knows about you. Mix up all the ones from the group and everyone draws one. Next, everyone has to guess who it belongs to.

11. Share your favorite sports team(s).

12. What is your favorite hobby/activity that makes you get lost for hours?

13. What is your favorite barbecue side?

14. What is your favorite flower and why?

15. What did you want to be when you "grew up"?

16. Are you a banana split, double scoop, or sundae lady?

17. Are you an entrepreneur or a 9-5er?

18. Who is your favorite superhero (male or female)?

19. What inspires you?

20. Do you prefer flip-flops or sandals?

21. Would you choose roller skating or rollerblading?

22. Would you prefer to go hiking or running?

23. Do you like sunsets or sunrises?

24. What is your favorite drink on a cold winter night?

25. What is your favorite movie of all time?

26. What is one thing that makes you unexplainably happy?

27. What is the favorite song you ever danced to?

28. Where would you spend your life if you could?

29. What season do you enjoy the most? Fall, winter, spring, or summer?

AFTER THE EVENT CHECKLIST

A few things to think about...

LOGISTICS

- ○ How many attendees did you have, and were there any new attendees? If so, did you introduce yourself and get their contact information?

- ○ Was the venue set up and ready to go on time?

- ○ Were there enough materials for everyone?

- ○ Did your venue work for your group?

- ○ If you served appetizers or other food items did you have enough?

- ○ Virtual event: Were you set up and ready to go on time?

- ○ Virtual event: What are some ways you engaged the attendees to keep their attention throughout the event (e.g. polls, utilized reaction buttons for responses, asking the attendees questions etc.)?

EXPECTATIONS/TAKEAWAYS:

○ Did the event meet your expectations? Why or why not?

○ Were your event goals reached?

○ What are three things you took away from the event?

FEEDBACK/FUTURE PLANNING:

○ Was there anything else that you determined was a future need for your group during this event?

○ Did anyone show interest in helping on the planning side for your group?

○ Is there anything you can do better the next time around?

○ What feedback did you receive from your follow-up surveys? For workshops/webinars, you can do a pre & a post-event survey to gauge what their takeaways were.

By the end of this book, you will have learned:

○ A variety of ways to encourage the women in your group.

○ Ways for your group to stay connected.

○ The importance of taking time to care for the Planner, that's you!

Chapter 1

PAMPER ME DAY

Okay, this is a day to pamper the ladies! Let's unwind!

CHAPTER 1

PAMPER ME DAY

Today we are encouraging health, relaxation, & well-being.

A FEW WEEKS BEFORE:

○ Choose your date and location.

○ Decide if you want to invite someone to do facials or 15-minute massages and set up the appointment.

○ Send a cute invitation out to everyone. These can be paper or evites done online.

○ Include a note in the invite for everyone to wear some cute flip-flops for the flip-flop fashion show.

○ Confirm the guests that will be coming to your Pamper Me Day.

○ Purchase some dry erase boards or cute cards to write on for scoring the flip-flop fashion show.

○ Plan your event takeaways. Some examples are:

  ▶ Rest
  ▶ Relaxation
  ▶ Providing healthy snack bag options with sample healthy snacks and a card with other easy ideas
  ▶ Encouraging everyone to take care of themselves
  ▶ Takeaway tips on simple stretches, exercises, stress-reducing tips, and the importance of taking care of your mental health.

TAKEAWAY TIPS:

○ Each morning write out your top three items to accomplish that day

○ Go for a walk

○ At the end of the day write out three things that you are grateful for

○ Break large tasks/projects into smaller tasks

○ Plan out simple spa recipes that can be prepared at home:

Lavender + Mint Bath Salts
Recipe taken from wellnessmama.com

○ **Ingredients**

- ► 2 cups Epsom salts
- ► ½ cup baking soda
- ► ¼ cup dead sea salt
- ► 30 drops of lavender essential oil
- ► 10 drops of peppermint essential oil
- ► 2 Tablespoons oil of choice: coconut, almond, jojoba, argan etc.

○ Instructions

1. Mix all ingredients in a medium size bowl.

2. Store in an air-tight jar and use ¼ cup per bath.

A FEW DAYS BEFORE:

○ Purchase the ingredients for the beauty treatments that everyone will be making.

○ Purchase small manicure or pedicure sets and some fun nail polish colors.

○ Purchase or make some light snacks like: fruit, yogurt, fresh veggies, hummus, and quiche to munch on.

○ Pick up a few small prizes for the flip-flop fashion show.

○ Prepare some of the beauty treatments & store in an airtight container.

DAY OF:

Prepare some infused waters to keep everyone hydrated. Choose one or two options below.

SOME IDEAS:

◆ **Strawberry slices & mint leaves:** 1 liter cold water, 8 oz. strawberries sliced, handful of mint leaves, ice.

◆ **Cucumber slices:** 1 liter cold water, 1 cucumber sliced, ice.

◆ **Berries & basil leaves:** 1 liter cold water, 16 oz. mixed berries (strawberries, blueberries, raspberries, blackberries etc.), a handful of basil, ice. Note: Do not overdo the basil as it can have a strong taste in the overall infused water. You could also replace the basil with mint leaves.

◆ **Orange slices & blueberries:** 1 liter cold water, 1 orange sliced, 16 oz. blueberries, ice.

◆ **Pomegranate seeds, ginger & lime slices:** 1 liter cold water, 3 limes sliced, 1 cup pomegranate seeds, small piece of peeled and finely grated ginger, ice.

◆ **Mixed berries:** 1 liter cold water, 16 oz. of berries, ice.

◆ **Cranberries & orange slices:** 1 liter cold water, 1 orange sliced, 16 oz. fresh cranberries, ice.

Choose organic fruits and herbs when you can. Wash them well in cold water. You can slice the strawberries, peel and slice the citrus or leave the rind on, and tear or crush a handful of fresh herb leaves. For the other berries, you can slightly crush them (you can pierce the cranberries down the center). The pomegranate seeds can be slightly crushed. Add your choice fruits and herbs (if using) to a large pitcher and pour ice cold water over the top of them. Add ice cubes. Infuse water at room temperature for no more than two hours. Put the water in the fridge to prevent bacterial growth. If you are making the infused waters in advance, replace the fruit with fresh fruit before serving for looks.

- ○ Turn on some relaxing tunes.

- ○ Arrange the snacks and infused waters for everyone.

- ○ Lay out the ingredients for the beauty treatments that everyone will be making along with small jars or other containers to put the finished products in.

- Have lots of towels available. You can prepare some warm, damp face or hand towels and store in a crockpot that has been turned to low. Put a little warm water on the bottom to keep towels moist. Check on them periodically to ensure there is still water remaining and replace accordingly. You can pass these out at the beginning of the event. Have your group drop these into a basket to dispose of.

- Have a basket at the door to drop phones in before entering the relaxation zone.

- Let everyone pamper themselves, or if someone will be doing facials or mini-massages, have a sign-up sheet ready with timed sessions marked out.

SOME IDEAS:

- **Facial Station:** Lay out pre-cut cucumber slices on a nice tray, have a package of make-up wipes available, along with a mirror, face mask packets and warm, damp towels.

- **Manicure/Pedicure Station:** Arrange the following nicely on a tray: Nail polish remover, mini nail or pedicure kits (one per person), several nice nail polish colors, a small bowl or basket of cotton balls, moisturizing lotion.

○ At each station, have a takeaway tip for a self-care topic. For example:

  ▶ By the snack area, have cards available to take with a list of healthy snack ideas.

  ▶ At the facial station have some tips for good mental health like reducing stress, surrounding yourself with good people, exercising, getting enough sleep, and quieting your mind.

  ▶ At the manicure/pedicure station have some tips available for good hand, arm, or overall body stretches.

○ Host the flip-flop fashion show. Hand out the dry erase boards or cute cards for everyone to write their scores on. Everyone will get a chance to walk the catwalk to show off their flip-flops if they want to!

○ Enjoy encouraging everyone to take care of themselves!

HOW TO CHANGE IT TO A VIRTUAL EVENT:

○ Choose your virtual platform option.

○ Send a virtual invitation or email with the link/password to the event, the ingredients for the spa recipe and infused water, and healthy snack ideas.

○ Encourage the group to choose a relaxing virtual background.

○ The host can play relaxing music through the virtual platform.

○ You can either mail out a mini Pamper Me Kit to each group member prior to the event based on how many register or have everyone prepare their own pamper me items and schedule different activities during certain times.

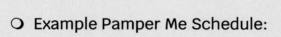

○ Example Pamper Me Schedule:

  ► 10:00 AM: Preparing infused water

  ► 10:30 AM: Facial station

  ► 11:15 AM: Mani/Pedi station

○ Encourage the group to participate in the virtual flip-flop fashion show.

○ Have fun!

SPOTLIGHT:

Encourage everyone to find time to care for themselves. Taking care of others and just the everyday hustle can be so taxing, and stress can be very destructive on our minds and bodies. It is important to take time to replenish, recharge, rejuvenate, and reboot your body, mind and spirit. Take a quick walk around the block or on the treadmill, go for a hike or run, or do a kettlebell workout. Find a workout that will meet your needs and get to it. Smile, relax and unwind every once in a while. It is good for the heart, the soul and the mind. Lastly, remember today to relax a little yourself.

PLANNER CARE:

Okay! So you have planned out your Pamper Me Day, you've sent out your invites, purchased a few things and snacks, and now you are ready to party! 30 minutes to an hour before your party, take a few minutes to:

- ○ Freshen up
- ○ Take a breath
- ○ Pray
- ○ Sit down for a minute
- ○ Reflect on the fact that as a leader you need to replenish, rejuvenate, and step away for a while every now and then. It's difficult to take care of others if you are not taking care of yourself. Set a date to do something that you enjoy.

FIND A WORKOUT THAT YOU CAN DO AT LEAST 3-4 DAYS A WEEK. WRITE OUT YOUR PLAN FOR THE WEEK HERE:

SUNDAY _____

MONDAY _____

TUESDAY _____

WEDNESDAY _____

THURSDAY _____

FRIDAY _____

SATURDAY _____

WRITE YOUR DATE HERE:

DATE _____

PUT ON YOUR FLIP FLOPS AND GET READY TO PARTY!

LAUGHTER, CHATTER & CHOCOLATE

A CHOCOLATE SOIREE

This is an evening in celebration of all things chocolate

CHAPTER 2

LAUGHTER, CHATTER & CHOCOLATE
-A CHOCOLATE SOIREE

In celebration of one of life's greatest candies, chocolate, we honor you. This evening is a celebration of all things chocolate, and laughter really is the best medicine, enjoy!

A FEW WEEKS BEFORE:

○ Choose your date and location.

○ Send a fun invitation out to everyone. These can be paper or evites done online and can embrace the chocolate theme. (See example invitation). Include a note in the invite for everyone to bring their favorite chocolate dessert or item.

○ Plan your event takeaways.

SOME EXAMPLES ARE:

► The importance of having fun every once in a while
► Enjoying chocolate - nothing beats that!
► Some kind of giveaway like chocolate covered popcorn, chocolate recipes, chocolate something
► The importance of taking care of your heart
► Comradery
► Encouraging fun and taking your mind off the daily hustle

○ Start planning a few games or activities.

HERE ARE A FEW IDEAS
(CHOOSE ONE OR A FEW OF THESE):

GUARD YOUR HEART GAME

(encouraging heart health both spiritually and physically):

Tie into the topic of heart disease for women. Offer some resources on heart awareness. Have heart-shaped sticky notes and baby clothespins ready or you can make hearts out of felt and attach with safety pins. Throughout the game you have to guard your heart. You cannot say the word Chocolate. If someone says the word and someone else hears them, that person can steal the other's heart. The winner with the most hearts at the end wins a prize. We experience and go through so much as women. It's important to guard what you allow into your space, mind, and spirit. It can affect all that you do.

"Keep your heart with all diligence, For out of it spring the issues of life."

Proverbs 4:23 NKJV

INVITATION IDEA:

CHOCOLATE COVERED APPLES:

Please note: These can be made in advance or at the beginning of your party to allow the chocolate time to set. Melt semisweet chocolate (either chips or pieces) in a bowl, stirring every once in a while until smooth and dip the apples. Have a few toppings like chopped nuts, shredded coconut, crushed candy pieces, etc. to roll them in right after dipping them in the chocolate. Set on waxed paper for a few hours to firm up. They can be packaged in clear party bags or wrapped with clear plastic wrap with a ribbon to tie closed.

TASTING PARTY:

Have samples of different types of chocolate available (have a range from white to dark chocolate, and maybe a specialty chocolate available like chocolate with bacon bits, caramel, or chilies) and create a scorecard for each woman.

POPCORN STATION

Arrange the following in your popcorn station:

- ▶ Melted white chocolate or dark chocolate to drizzle (can be put in a mini crockpot to keep warm)
- ▶ Pre-popped popcorn in a large bowl with a large spoon or ladle to scoop the popcorn
- ▶ Cute party bags to put the popcorn in
- ▶ Toppings (such as sprinkles, small dried fruit pieces, candy assortment, pretzels, or nuts)
- ▶ Tags to write the name of their original mix or to put their name on it.

A CHOCOLATE FOUNTAIN IS A MUST!

Decide what items you will dip in the fountain. Some examples of items to dip: Strawberries, pineapple spears, sliced bananas, pretzel spears, marshmallows, pound cake chunks, rice crispy treats on a stick, or other fresh fruit.

A FEW DAYS BEFORE:

○ Shop for your chocolate for the fountain and items to dip in the fountain.

○ Shop for a few other non-chocolate snacks.

○ Finalize your games or activities.

DAY OF:

○ Have the fountain ready to go when everyone arrives. Nothing beats the aroma of warm chocolate! Surround the fountain with the items to dip in colorful bowls.

○ Have some other non-chocolate snacks available for munching and some palate cleansers like lemon water or slices of apple.

○ Get your games going.

○ Enjoy, and have some fun!

WE'VE SAMPLED CHOCOLATE CAKES, COOKIES, ICE CREAM, FONDUE, CANDY, CHEESECAKES, & PIES. WE'VE DIPPED ASSORTED FRUITS, MARSHMALLOWS, POUND CAKE CUBES, AND EVEN POTATO CHIPS!

DULCE DE LECHE AND CHOCOLATE GRANITA
– BY CHEF AFIYA GRIFFITH

INGREDIENTS:

2 cups whole milk, ½ cup sugar, 1/3 cup natural cocoa powder, 4 teaspoons cornstarch, 3 large egg yolks, 2 teaspoons pure vanilla extract

DIRECTIONS:

Dulce de leche sauce: Put 1 ½ cups of the milk, the sugar, and the cocoa in a nonreactive (stainless steel) saucepan. Bring to a simmer, over medium-high heat. Remove from heat.

Chocolate pudding: Meanwhile, whisk the remaining ½ cup of the milk, cornstarch, salt, egg yolks, and vanilla in a bowl. Gradually whisk the hot milk into the egg mixture. Return to the saucepan and cook over medium-high heat whisking constantly, until the pudding comes to a full boil. Reduce the heat to maintain a simmer, and continue whisking until thick, about 2 or 3 minutes. Pour in ½ Dulce de leche sauce. Stir with chocolate pudding and pour in a casserole dish. Let set for 20 minutes. Take out, fluff surface with a fork. Repeat every 20 minutes until the entire dish is in granita form. After the last fork fluff, take a spoon and serve in a sundae glass with desired ice cream toppings (preferably chocolate sauce or caramel).

TIPS TO HELP GROW YOUR GROUP:

This is a great party to invite new women to. Invite a friend, a family member, or a co-worker. The only requirement is that they bring their favorite chocolate dessert or dish to share. Break the ice by having everyone choose a random letter out of a bowl and write down one word that they feel describes chocolate that begins with that letter. Once everyone has their word, they will have a chance to read it aloud. The fun is that they now will use the word they wrote to tell the group something about themselves. Games are great to break the ice and get everyone up laughing, cheering each other on, and having some friendly fun.

A little friendly competition helps to build friendships, and if everyone is having fun they may invite a friend to join the next time. I have learned that there is no such thing as too much chocolate! The possibilities are endless! We've sampled chocolate cakes, cookies, ice cream, fondue, candy, cheesecakes, & pies. We've dipped assorted fruits, marshmallows, pound cake cubes, and even potato chips! Enjoy yourself and embrace the chocolate!

"Oh, taste and see that the Lord is good; Blessed is the man who trusts in Him!"

Psalm 34:8 NKJV

HOW TO CHANGE IT TO A VIRTUAL EVENT:

○ Choose your virtual platform option.

○ Send a virtual invitation or email with the link/password to the soiree, and instructions to shop for ingredients for one of the activities that can be done virtually. For example:

    ○ Shop for candy apple ingredients: green apples, either milk or dark chocolate, toppings that will stick to the chocolate as you roll the apple in them, and sticks to put the apples on.

    ○ Shop for chocolate tasting party ingredients: 3 - 4 types of chocolate to fit the categories e.g. Dark chocolate, milk chocolate, specialty chocolate, white chocolate, etc.

○ Plan for a few virtual games/activities that can incorporate the chocolate theme.

○ Have fun!

Tasting Scorecard

Take notes on the following under each chocolate tasting: What is the texture, taste, and feel of the chocolate in your mouth. Which one was your favorite?

1 2 3

4 5 6

PLANNER CARE:

Okay! So you have planned out your Chocolate Soiree, you've sent out your invites, set up your chocolate fountain and treats, and now you are ready to party! 30 minutes to an hour before your party, take a few minutes to:

- ○ Freshen up
- ○ Take a breath
- ○ Sit down for a minute
- ○ Step Away Moments: It is easy to get burned out, even with a great team. It can take a lot out of you emotionally, mentally and spiritually to lead other women. Think of some ways to "step away" every now and then, even if just to pray for yourself and your group. You could use some of the ideas from the Girl's Day or Night Out activities in Chapter 4 to get you started.

DRAW YOUR IDEAS HERE:

FIND SOMEONE WHO CAN KEEP YOU LIFTED UP IN PRAYER. LIST THEIR NAME HERE AND REACH OUT TO THEM THIS WEEK:

DIP A TREAT IN CHOCOLATE, ENJOY IT, AND GET READY TO PARTY!

Chapter 3

THEMED TALKS

There are certain foods like tacos, french fries, and ice cream that I absolutely love. This activity combines topics of interest with favorite foods for an afternoon or evening of fun.

CHAPTER 3

THEMED TALKS

Favorite foods + drinks + friendship = A recipe for fun

A FEW WEEKS BEFORE:

Create two sets of cards or slips of paper, one for everyone in your group to write their topic(s) of interest on, and one for them to write their favorite food item on. Put these in two separate jars.

Here are some topic ideas:

1. Friendship
2. Encouragement
3. Prayer
4. Mentoring
5. Self-Empowerment
6. Laughter
7. Self-Worth
8. Forgiveness
9. Marriage
10. Movies
11. Role of the Woman
12. Networking
13. Body Image & Eating Disorders
14. Caregiving
15. Destiny
16. Sports
17. Dating
18. Books
19. TV Shows
20. College
21. Goals
22. Motherhood
23. Talents
24. Submission

25. Temptation

26. Time Management

27. Codependency

28. Mental Health

29. Empty Nest

30. Gossip

31. Health

32. Personal Finance

33. Entrepreneurship

34. Leadership

35. Career Exploration

36. Food

37. Running

38. The Future

39. Art

○ Decide on the topic and favorite food that will be served at the talk by drawing one card out of each jar. Depending on the favorite food, you can either have everyone bring a part of the meal. For example, if tacos are the favorite food, someone can bring taco shells, someone else can bring some meat, cheese, salsa, etc.; or if the favorite food is a dessert like cheesecake, everyone can bring a type of cheesecake for the group to sample.

○ Send out a fun invitation or spread by word of mouth.

Example: You are invited to our "List favorite food choice Talks" event

○ You can create an activity or game around your theme.

Here are a few examples:

▶ **Goals:** Have everyone create a goal or vision board. Encourage everyone to bring a few magazines to create their goal or vision board. Provide blank cardstock or poster board for the base of the vision board.

► **Friendship:** Have everyone create a friendship bracelet to give to a friend. Provide an assortment of colors of string, scissors, and instructions on how to create the bracelets. You could also provide little bags to package the bracelets in, and a tag to write the friend's name on.

► **Finances:** Provide a 30-day tracking sheet or share a few free phone or online apps that can help with tracking spending. Encourage everyone to track their income and expenses over the next 30 days. Set a day to meet again and have the group identify items on their list that are needs vs. items that are wants. Use this list as a guide for them to build their budget. Provide the basics on what is included in a budget and work with the group to create their own personal budget.

► **Mentoring:** This works well with a group that is a part of a larger group. Prior to the event, collect contact information, interests, and each prospective mentee's input on why they would like a mentor. From those who would like to be a mentor, collect a mentorship application with information such as: why they want to be a mentor, what skills and gifts they have that they could share, what hobbies they have, and what their occupation is. It is also a great idea to have them sign a confidentiality agreement, and complete a background check. Pair the mentors with the mentees and host an initial "Meet Your Mentee" event. You could also host several overall Mentor/Mentee meetups throughout a certain time period.

► **Movies:** Choose a favorite movie to watch together. Encourage everyone to bring movie-themed snacks like popcorn, their favorite candy, fixings for a nacho bar, etc. Provide drinks like sparkling water and or soft drinks.

A FEW DAYS BEFORE:

○ Confirm what everyone in your group will be bringing.

○ Shop for any last minute items or groceries.

○ Ensure that the host will have beverages for the group. Depending on the season the beverages can be lemonade, punch, coffee & tea, or water.

○ Finalize any handouts or takeaways that you would like everyone to take home. Prepare some questions to trigger discussion around the topic of choice.

DAY OF:

○ Set up the area where the food and beverages will be placed.

○ Encourage the group to place their phones in a basket during the event.

○ Remind everyone of the topic and that the focus of the day is on the topic.

○ When everyone has their food, open up with the first question.

○ Have fun!

EXAMPLE TOPIC: FRIENDSHIP

Example Questions:

► How do you choose a friend or what are qualities of a good friend?

► Have you ever felt the need to befriend someone you did not like?

► Have you ever found yourself in a toxic friend situation? What did you do?

► How would you define a friend?

► Is it easy for you to forgive a friend?

HOW TO CHANGE IT TO A VIRTUAL EVENT:

○ Choose your virtual platform option.

○ Create an event virtual background that everyone can load on their own computer/ phone for the event with your group color, photo, and/or event topic.

○ Send a virtual invitation or email with the link/password to the talk, topic for the day and favorite food item for them to purchase or prepare.

○ Encourage the group to take part in both the topic and favorite food. You could even all order from the same restaurant or food vendor prior to the event.

○ Plan your activities/discussions around your topic. For example:

▶ **Art:** Have everyone purchase a small canvas and watercolors. During the event, plan time to paint a certain picture with the group.

▶ **Finances:** Email a few budgeting worksheets with savings goal cards you make out to the group with the invite.

▶ **Virtual Vision Board Party**: Host a virtual vision board party. More about this in Chapter 12.

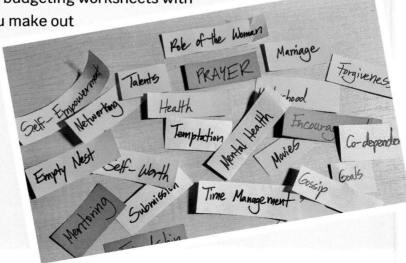

TIPS TO HELP GROW YOUR GROUP:

It is important to develop a safe environment for those attending group meetings or outings to feel comfortable sharing within the group. What is shared in the group stays within the group. Many things can break down group dynamics, but an environment that is not safe to share opinions, worries or issues for fear that it will be spread outside of the group is high on the list. Establish a safe environment and watch your group grow.

PLANNER CARE:

Okay! So you have planned out your Themed Talk, you've sent out your invites, purchased a few snacks, and now you're ready to party! 30 minutes to an hour before your party, take a few minutes to:

○ Freshen up

○ Take a breath

○ Pray: Write out a quick prayer for yourself here:

○ Stretch

○ Sit down for a minute

○ Enjoy a cold or warm beverage depending on the season and get ready to party!

PERSONAL THEME:

You have a word and food item set for today, now it's time to choose a word that will describe your own goals and your vision for this year. I've found that choosing a word helps to set a direction for your year that can help you move closer to your goals. Some examples of some words I've used in the past include: Encouraged, Grateful, Courageous, Determined, and Inspired. A few other words you might use are: Focused, Appreciative, Powerful, Fearless, and Driven. Use your word to help create focus, and define it so you know what you are trying to accomplish. Think about how this word will help you accomplish this task or how this word will help motivate you to reach this goal. How will this word fit into your story? For example:

THEME WORD = FEARLESS:

Some questions to ask yourself:

1. What goals have you delayed due to a fear of failure, lack of resources, or some other factor?

2. What steps would you take to reach these goals if nothing was holding you back? You may need to do some research here to determine what is needed to get from point A to point B.

3. Who can help you accomplish your goals? This can be someone already working in the field that you want to work in, a mentor or an online resource or expert that can help you take steps towards your goals.

4. How can you set goals including your date of completion to represent your word and what action items can you write down today?

5. At the end of the year, what results would make you feel that you have lived your fearless year? Start working towards it!

6. Create a few planner spreads that incorporate your theme word in your planner throughout the year as a reminder of what you are working towards.

GIRL'S DAY OR NIGHT OUT

Grab some friends and head out for a day or night out with the girls

CHAPTER 4

GIRL'S DAY OR NIGHT OUT

Have you wanted to try a new restaurant, paint a picture during an art night, or go see a movie that just came out? Let's do something fun!

A FEW WEEKS BEFORE:

- ○ Choose your activity or event. Here are some ideas to get you started:

    - ▶ Choose a favorite restaurant
    - ▶ Attend a local sporting event
    - ▶ Take a cooking class
    - ▶ Get creative at an Art night
    - ▶ Let's have some competitive fun at a game night
    - ▶ Find something fun to do in a city close by
    - ▶ Go on a shopping trip
    - ▶ Visit a spa for some pampering
    - ▶ Check out a movie that just came out
    - ▶ Go for a run or hike together
    - ▶ Go to a new restaurant for brunch or dessert only

- ○ Send out an invitation to everyone including the time, where you will meet, contact person etc.

- ○ If your group has specific t-shirts, hats, or another item to identify your group, invite everyone to wear that item on the day or night out.

DAY OF:

- ○ Carpool to or meet at the event destination.
- ○ Have fun and take lots of pictures.

AFTER THE ACTIVITY OR EVENT:

- ○ Create a group scrapbook with the event pictures.

HOW TO CHANGE IT TO A VIRTUAL EVENT:

- ○ Choose your virtual platform option.
- ○ Choose an activity you can do virtually. For example:
  - ▶ Cooking class: Send the recipe cards out with the invite so everyone can purchase the ingredients.
  - ▶ Art Night: Send a list of art supplies to buy with the invite.
  - ▶ Watch a movie: Host a virtual movie night. Send a link to the shared movie to the group.
- ○ Create an event virtual background that everyone can load on their own computer/phone for the event with your group color, photo, and/or event topic.
- ○ Send a virtual invitation or email with the link/password to the day or night out.
- ○ Encourage the group to wear any group SWAG they have (t-shirts, hats etc.).
- ○ Take a snapshot of the virtual event with everyone in their group SWAG.
- ○ Have fun!

SPOTLIGHT:

Sometimes it's nice to step away from the daily hustle to do something different. Choose an activity and have some fun! Make some lifelong memories, sip your favorite cold brew, and enjoy the company. You may discover the competitive or creative side of some of your attendees, or find a new shopping buddy. During these group events, there is time to get to know your group. Every group member brings something to the overall group. Encourage your group to utilize their talents, and share their interests or hobbies. This will not only help them grow, but it can help to build the overall group. If someone is good at baking, they might be willing to bake a cake or other dessert for an event. If someone is a planner they may be able to help coordinate activities for the group. Everyone is a part of the team.

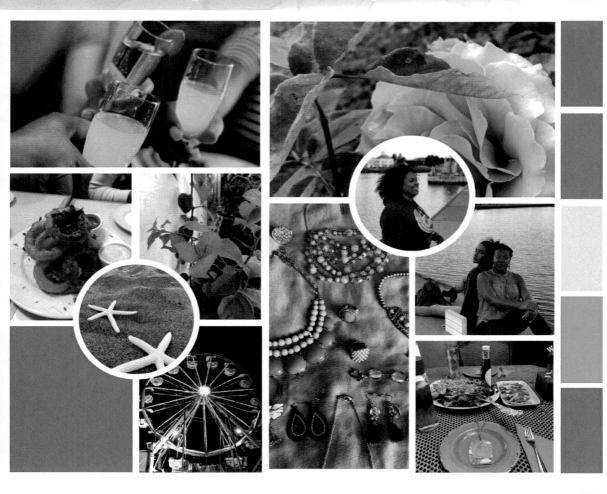

PLANNER CARE:

Okay! So you have planned your Girl's Day or Night Out and you are ready to venture out on the town! 30 minutes to an hour before your day or night out, take a few minutes to:

○ Sit down for a minute

○ Review the directions to the outing destination

○ Be encouraged: Sometimes as leaders we want everyone to get involved. Through the years I've learned that some members come and go, some stay, and some come once and never come back. Be encouraged that whoever is there is meant to be there. Focus on encouraging those that do come. Write out one way to encourage yourself here and work on that this month (check out Chapter 14 for some ideas):

I WILL ENCOURAGE MYSELF BY:

3 WAYS TO TAKE ACTION ON IT THIS MONTH:

01

02

03

GRAB YOUR CAMERA OR CAMERA PHONE AND LET'S HAVE FUN!

WHAT IF...

Life happens... here are a few ways to prepare, plan in advance, and get back on track if:

A CATERER RUNS LATE:

► A few days prior, call the caterer and confirm the address & time of your event.

► During setup provide a bowl of mints/candies at each table.

► Apologize to the attendees, and keep them in the loop. Do a quick review of your event activities, and if possible do an additional activity until the food arrives.

ATTENDEES ARE RUNNING LATE:

► Create excitement for your event in the days leading up to the event through electronic notifications, emails etc. You could even do a virtual event countdown on your webpage.

► Send a reminder notification to your participants the night before.

► On the morning of your event, review your event goals and the timeframe you have set for each activity.

► Utilize some of the planner care ideas until the attendees come.

► Depending on how late they come, readjust your schedule, ensuring that you will still meet the event goals you set. For example, if you previously had two or three activities planned, but you can still accomplish your goals with one or two activities, cut an activity or two.

YOU ARE SHORT ON FOOD/SUPPLIES:

- ▶ Prior to the event, if possible, get a count of attendees and plan for an additional X amount of people depending on your budget. It is always better to have a little extra than not enough especially when it comes to food.
- ▶ Identify locations close to your event where you could purchase a few sandwich/dessert trays if needed.

THE SPEAKER IS RUNNING LATE:

- ▶ Prior to the event make sure you have a good contact phone number for your speaker and that they have your information. Reach out to the speaker the day before to confirm any last details and check-in.
- ▶ Prep an activity or two that you can have as a backup to help make good use of your attendee's time and still meet your event goals.
- ▶ On the day of the event, move activities around on your schedule if needed.

SET UP IS RUNNING BEHIND:

- ▶ Prep the refreshment area first, especially if attendees will enjoy these at the beginning of your event. Put some music on and encourage the attendees to mingle and talk while you utilize a few extra minutes to get ready.
- ▶ Utilize your planning team to help get any last minute items resolved.

ADDITIONAL ATTENDEES SHOW UP:

- ▶ Always prep for a few extra attendees.
- ▶ Have attendees register for larger events. This could be through a contact person or through an event planning site where attendees can register for your event.
- ▶ Have a backup plan in place: Either a game or interactive activity that everyone can join in regardless of materials.

YOU FORGOT TO CREATE A MUSIC PLAYLIST FOR YOUR EVENT:

- ▶ Utilize a music app or pre-made online playlist.

TECHNOLOGY IS GIVING YOU THE BLUES:

- ▶ Prior to the event, designate a co-host. This person can take the lead on a virtual event until you are connected again.
- ▶ Plan to have a backup for your internet like a hotspot.
- ▶ If you get disconnected from one device, try another. You can log into the virtual platform from a desktop, laptop, phone or other smart device.

Remember, planning ahead can help alleviate some of the worries about these potential what if scenarios. If they happen, relax and put your plan into action.

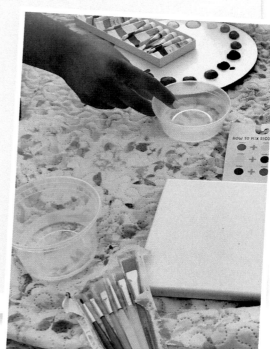

ANCHORED, FOCUSED & LOVED

WOMEN'S RETREAT

Through everything we experience in life, God is with us. He is the anchor! In him we can have peace of mind, from him we feel his great love for us, and because of him we know that we are not without hope because he lives!

CHAPTER 5

"ANCHORED, FOCUSED & LOVED"
-WOMEN'S RETREAT

(4-5 MONTHS TO A YEAR OUT):

- ○ Put a committee together to plan retreat details. This retreat has a sea theme! Get all the ideas down.
- ○ Choose your retreat dates and venue (e.g. Rent a vacation house or cabin, reserve rooms on a cruise etc.).
- ○ Choose your speaker and send a formal invitation to her.
- ○ Retreat Scriptures: Hebrews 6:19 NKJV, Romans 8:38-39 NKJV, Romans 10:9 NKJV.
- ○ Get the word out about your retreat.

SOME MARKETING IDEAS:

- ▶ Post a sign-up sheet.
- ▶ Use pictures from past retreats.
- ▶ Promote the retreat scriptures.
- ▶ Find pictures of the area where you will be hosting the retreat to utilize.
- ▶ Create special invitations or fliers with all the details to send out and post. See example invitation. Think about what information would be needed to plan for a few days.
- ▶ Advertise on social media or your group's webpage.

SET UP PAYMENT ARRANGEMENTS:

○ Can be monthly, biweekly, or the group can pay in full.

INVITATION IDEA:

PUT A MENU AND ITINERARY TOGETHER:

Some menu ideas:

○ Breakfast:
- ► Croissants
- ► Fresh seasonal fruit cups
- ► Jamila's broccoli cheese quiche – See page 93
- ► Scrambled eggs
- ► Freshly baked biscuits
- ► Sausage links, crispy applewood smoked bacon, or glazed ham slices
- ► Yogurt & granola
- ► Coffee, tea, OJ, apple juice

○ Lunch:

► Make your own sandwiches with condiments or provide pre-made sandwiches individually wrapped with individual condiments.

► Chip assortment (individually packaged)

► Fresh fruit salad (individually packaged)

► Cookie & brownie bar (individually wrapped)

► Assortment of drinks

○ Dinner:

► Three cheese Lasagna, spaghetti with meat sauce, or some delicious type of casserole

► Green salad with assorted toppings and dressings

► Garlic, cheese knots

► Fresh berries and whipped cream, lemon bars or tiramisu (my favorites)

► Assortment of drinks

A MONTH OUT:

○ Finalize your list of attendees.

○ Follow up with your speaker to see if there is anything she needs. (e.g. printouts or materials for activities, etc.)

○ Put takeaways and workbooks together to pass out the first day of the retreat. The workbooks can be put into a binder or professionally bound and put into a tote bag for everyone.

○ Plan out the Group Discussion and Chill Time topic ideas for this retreat:

ANCHORED DOWN:

Through everything we experience in life, God is with us. He is the anchor! Anchors keep their ships grounded. In Him we can have peace of mind, from Him we feel His great love for us, and because of Him we know that we are not without hope because He lives! We can always bring our issues and concerns to Him in prayer. Open up the group discussion with everyone placing an issue that they or someone they know is facing in a jar with or without names. Throughout the retreat have everyone offer a prayer over them at their leisure.

DISCONNECTED & DETACHED:

Life happens, but what do you do when you are going through? How do you encourage yourself so that you can encourage others? This will be an opportunity for some quiet time. Encourage everyone to use the journaling sheets included in their packets to study the listed scriptures and brainstorm ways to stay anchored and afloat. See Appendix A in the back of the book for more information.

NOT WITHOUT HOPE:

Retreat scripture: Hebrews 6:19 NKJV. Because of all God has done for us, we do not live as if we have no hope. Through life's ups and downs God is always with us. Our hope is in Him! Encourage the group to take some time to review the following stories in groups and meet back to discuss as an overall group. See Appendix B in the back of the book for more information.

LOOK UP... A DISCUSSION ON LOVE:

Retreat scripture: Romans 8:38-39 NKJV. This can be in the format of a group discussion. Prepare a few questions and scriptures around the topic of love. Bring strips of streamers to use during this activity. Give everyone a chance to write one thing they love about themselves or a scripture on God's love for us on their streamer and hang these expressions of love in an open area from a doorframe. Open the floor for a love discussion including the topics of self-love, love within relationships and God's love. His love for us is so amazing, all encompassing, and unending. If we ever forget this, just remember to look up. He is everywhere. Leave the streamers up throughout the retreat for the group to reflect on or add to.

○ Figure out what hands-on activities you will do during the retreat.

SOME FUN IDEAS FOR THIS RETREAT:

▶ **Anchors Away:** Have everyone write out on an item (I have used rocks or flat stones - or some item that will not cause pollution in the ocean or on the beach, and a permanent marker to write with) that will represent an anchor, things that they want to let go of or put behind them. At some time during the retreat they will release these anchors into the sea as a symbol of releasing them to God. "Therefore humble yourselves under the mighty hand of God, that He may exalt you in due time, casting all your care upon Him, for He cares for you." 1 Peter 5:6-7 NKJV

- ▶ **Vision/Hope Boards:** Without a vision of where you want to go, and what you want to do, it is easy to lose focus. Take some time to create a visual reminder of your dreams, goals and of what you feel your purpose is. After the retreat this will be something that everyone can hang up and reflect back on as they progress towards their dreams, goals and purpose. You can use paper that has anchors on it or a map for the background. Encourage the group to set specific dates to accomplish goals and to include a few action steps to reach that goal.
- ▶ **Anchor Journal:** Use template pages for the journal sheets, and provide supplies to decorate the cover. The journal can be put into the retreat binder or workbook as well.
- ▶ **Costume photo op:** Have different props available for everyone to pose with and have someone taking photos for keepsakes. You can go with the beach theme or have some other fun props.
- ▶ **Paint Night:** Choose a beach-themed picture to paint + a part of the retreat scripture on a canvas. E.g. From Romans 8:38 NKJV "For I am persuaded," since it is a long scripture.
- ▶ **Anchor Necklace:** Provide beads, anchor charms or hearts and necklace strands for everyone to create their necklace.
- ▶ **Anchor Picture Frame:** Provide a picture frame, and supplies to decorate it, including anchor charms.
- ○ Decide what your event takeaways will be:

SOME IDEAS:

- ► To realize that in God we are anchored & never shaken
- ► To realize that our hope is in God
- ► To make new friends
- ► To truly enjoy the retreat weekdays or weekend
- ► To be relaxed
- ► To have released something that may have been holding her back
- ► To get focused! There is work to do.
- ► Rejuvenation
- ► To learn tips on how to make life a little easier, her load a little lighter, etc.

○ Choose your decorations for the retreat. Some ideas: Beach buckets and shovels, life saver tubes, lighthouses, fishing nets, starfish, shells, sand, anchors, and bright colors.

WEEK BEFORE:

○ Pass out the itinerary with a list of items to bring and meet with everyone to answer any last questions.

○ Some items for everyone to bring include: Clothing based on the retreat location, a sturdy pair of walking shoes, a Bible, a desire to relax and grow spiritually.

○ Some items for you to bring include: Retreat food and drinks, a Bible, retreat booklets/folders/materials, some background music, clothes for a few days, a watch, stationary paper/colorful note paper to write notes on, and directions to the retreat.

○ Confirm driving arrangements and meeting location.

○ Finalize any last minute details with the venue.

FIRST DAY OF RETREAT:

○ Greet everyone and help them load their items into the vehicle(s).

○ Head out to retreat!

○ Introduce your speaker and have everyone introduce themselves in case there is anyone new.

○ Have fun!

JAMILA'S BROCCOLI CHEESE QUICHE

Preheat oven to 400 degrees Fahrenheit.

INGREDIENTS:

2 frozen Pastry Pie Shells (deep-dish), 2 tbsp. butter melted, ½ cup minced yellow onion sautéed in a little garlic olive oil, salt and pepper to taste, 8 eggs, 2 broccoli crowns, 1 ½ cups heavy cream, 1 package (1¼ cups) finely shredded Italian blend cheese (Shredded parmesan, Fontina, Asiago, & Romano cheese), ½ cup Mild Cheddar cheese finely shredded, ½ tsp of each: onion powder, garlic powder, cayenne pepper.

DIRECTIONS:

FOR CRUSTS:

Prick crust with a fork all over. Bake for 10 minutes. Take out and let cool for a few minutes then fill with filling. Do not overfill. Bake for 45 minutes covered loosely with foil. Remove foil and bake for an additional 12 minutes or until the quiche is set and the crust is golden brown. Please note baking time may vary depending on your oven. Remove from oven and allow to sit for 10 minutes. Enjoy!

FOR FILLING:

Separate the broccoli florets and place in boiling water for a few minutes until tender. Remove from water and drain. Chop into smaller pieces. Sauté onion in a skillet in a tbsp. of garlic olive oil until tender. Cool for a few minutes. In a mixing bowl, whisk eggs & heavy cream until combined. Stir in onions, cheese, seasonings to taste, broccoli, and cooled melted butter.

FOR SERVING:

This is delicious with a side of fruit salad of your favorite summer fruits or breakfast meat like sausage or bacon.

SPOTLIGHT:

Retreats are a great opportunity to get to know everyone in your group. I was really nervous planning my first retreat. I had been to several in the past, but I was now responsible for the logistics. Once I put together a plan of action, I was able to ask for help where needed, and break the list down into manageable tasks. Give yourself plenty of time and have fun. You are creating an experience that will offer time to rest, relax, and grow together in a fun environment. Feel free to create team building activities, opportunities to take time and be still before the Lord, and time to explore the area that you are in (after all, why retreat close to the beach and not enjoy a little sand and sun?). Through the years and through the retreats that I have attended and hosted, I have come to realize that God is my peace, my grace, my provider, my deliverer, my comforter, my strength, my life, my joy, and my rest. Nothing is too hard to do; after all,

"I can do all things through Christ who strengthens me."

Philippians 4:13 NKJV

HOW TO CHANGE IT TO A VIRTUAL EVENT:

○ Choose your virtual platform option.

○ Choose what format you will use: Either one day or two days with certain times to check in.

○ Create a virtual background for the retreat with the retreat theme on it for the group to upload.

○ Send a virtual invitation or email with the link/password to the retreat and retreat agenda for either one day or two days.

○ Encourage the group to wear comfortable clothing or group SWAG (t-shirts, hats etc.).

○ Do a poll at the beginning to see what your group wants to take away from this retreat.

○ Depending on your sessions, utilize the platform features like breakout rooms for different sessions that your group can sign-up for in advance through their registration.

○ Based on your activity choices, you can plan to send all necessary supplies out prior to the event. These can be placed in a tote bag and distributed to the group. Include some activities for virtual team building, like a group icebreaker. You can use the poll feature to ask the question and everyone has a chance to reply live.

○ For the retreat food everyone can either provide their own meals or you can organize a meal delivery from a specific restaurant to each attendee's home for specific meals like breakfast/lunch.

○ Any videos can be uploaded through the host's computer by sharing their screen.

○ The prayer list can stay open through a shared online document throughout the retreat.

○ Take pics of activities by taking a screenshot as the retreat is going to share later, and encourage the group to take photos of any projects to share with the group later on.

○ Have fun!

REST, RECHARGE, AND HAVE A LITTLE FUN...

PLANNER CARE:

Okay! So you have planned out your retreat, everyone has signed up, they are excited to go and will soon be arriving, and you've packed the trunk or van with the supplies you are bringing. 30 minutes to an hour before everyone starts arriving on the first morning of the retreat, take a few minutes to:

- ○ Freshen up

- ○ Take a breath

- ○ Pray over those that are attending the retreat that they will take away what they needed and that you will as well

- ○ Sit down for a minute

- ○ Write out why this retreat matters to you, and what encourages you to do it:

JOT DOWN A FEW THINGS THAT YOU WANT TO TAKE AWAY FROM THE RETREAT HERE:

Chapter 6

SUMMER BRUNCH

The days are longer and the weather is nice. Gather a few friends for a brunch!

CHAPTER 6

SUMMER BRUNCH

Tasty food + Fun environment + Great Company = Fun times.

A FEW WEEKS BEFORE

- ○ Choose your date and location.
- ○ Choose your theme:

SOME IDEAS:

- ▶ **Beach or surf theme:** Use beach toys, sand, seashells, netting, lighthouses, anchors, colorful straws, napkins, plates etc.
- ▶ **Sun dresses and flip-flops:** Colorful straws, napkins, drink umbrellas and fun décor, flip-flops, sundresses, sun hats.
- ▶ **Favorite chick flick:** Have everyone dress in and decorate in the theme of the movie.
- ▶ **Summer bucket list:** Have everyone bring or wear something that represents an item on their summer bucket list. You could assign tables prior to the event and have everyone decorate their table for their theme.
- ▶ **Barbecue or picnic:** Can use picnic baskets, gingham patterned tablecloths, wicker plate trays, fake ants, watermelon.
- ▶ **Luau theme:** Flower Leis either with artificial or real flowers, seashells, Hula skirts, Hawaiian dresses or shirts, flowers, pineapples, coconut shells for drinks, colorful straws, drink umbrellas, Tropicana or sun hats.

- ▶ **Flowers:** Choose a few types and you can use either artificial or real flowers. If anyone has allergies, you may want to use artificial flowers. Place in different sized or similar sized vases and place around the venue.
- ▶ **Summer Camp:** Tents, lanterns, sleeping bags, marshmallows, s'mores, fake ants, "Don't feed the bears" signs, campfire setup (can use real wood and make fake flames from red, orange, and yellow tissue paper).
- ▶ **Ice Cream Party:** All types of ice cream treats and toppings, ice cream cones, waffle bowls, cute ice cream bowls, colorful spoons, a few ice cream scoops.
- ▶ **Fit & Fabulous:** Have everyone wear their favorite workout gear, decorate with exercise gear: jump ropes, weights, gloves, hats, exercise mats or blocks, tape measures, pedometers, cute socks, health journals, drawstring bags, hand sanitizers, healthy recipes, breast cancer awareness or heart health awareness giveaway items, exercise bands, terry cloth wristbands, colorful plates, napkins, water bottles instead of cups, several types of infused water in dispensers or clear pitchers.
- ○ Send a fun invitation out to everyone. These can be paper or evites done online (See example invitation).

INVITATION IDEA:

Fit & Fab
Brunch
15 SCOTTS LANE
JUNE 23

○ Include a note in the invitation to come dressed comfortably or in the brunch theme.

○ Choose a menu or have everyone bring their favorite item.

Sample menu brought to you by Chef Afiya Griffith:

FIT & FABULOUS SUMMER BRUNCH:

- ► Whole Wheat Coconut Pancakes
- ► Chicken Sausage and Egg White Frittata
- ► Berry Blast Fruit Shooters
- ► Roasted Garlic Smashed Red Potatoes
- ► Marinated Tomato and Cucumber Salad
- ► Ricotta and Jam Toast

JAMILA'S SUMMERTIME PASTA SALAD

INGREDIENTS:

1 orange or yellow sweet bell pepper rinsed and diced medium cut, 1 medium can sliced black olives drained, 1 cup of Kalamata olives cut in half, 2 cups mixed cherry tomatoes (yellow and red) rinsed and cut in half, box of rotini pasta cooked until tender but not squishy, 1 container of fresh marinated mozzarella balls drained and sliced into thirds (I add the seasoning at the bottom of the container as well), jar of Caesar salad dressing.

DIRECTIONS:

Let the cooked pasta cool until it is no longer boiling hot. Combine veggies with pasta and mozzarella. Pour Caesar salad dressing over everything and mix well. Refrigerate for a few hours to blend the flavors. Enjoy!

Note: You could also add meat to this dish such as diced ham or diced salami chunks to make a heartier dish.

- ▶ Choose at least one activity or game that encompasses your theme. These can be used as icebreaker activities as well.

HERE ARE A FEW IDEAS:

- ○ **Beach Trip Showdown:** All items will start out in two beach bags including the floaters which the teams will need to inflate. The two beach bags will be filled with items you would wear or carry to the beach. These can include: A beach wrap or cover-up, flip-flops, beach hat, sunscreen, arm floaties, beach blanket, lip balm, sunglasses, towel, goggles, light sweater or jacket, umbrella, and a lifeguard whistle. Each team has two minutes to put as many items as possible on their "beachgoer." The first team to blow their whistle wins.

- ○ **Luau theme:** Host a hula hoop or a limbo contest. You can have a special Luau-themed drink bar set up. The type of drink will be determined by the crowd.

FUN ACTIVITY: MAKING A TROPICAL LEI:

- ▶ Lay out base items: Ribbon, sturdy thin cord, needle to thread flowers.
- ▶ Lay out a selection of flowers (either real or imitation) that can be threaded on your ribbon or cord.
- ▶ To make your lei: Thread your flowers on your lei and tie your ribbon or cord at the end to close it.

- ○ **Summer Camp:** Set up a s'more bar complete with Bunsen burners to roast the marshmallows, graham crackers, mini chocolate bars (for gourmet s'mores you can use a variety of chocolate bars), and marshmallow roasting sticks (metal skewers or wood skewers that have been soaked in water).

- ○ **Ice Cream Party:** Set up an ice cream sundae bar complete with ice cream cones, waffle bowls, fresh fruit, crushed nuts, whipped cream, Maraschino cherries, sprinkles, hot fudge, strawberry and caramel sauce and any other favorite toppings.

WEEK OF:

- ○ Confirm who will be attending.
- ○ Pull out some nice serveware & plates or find some nice paperware.
- ○ Print out or write on a few store bought food signs like mini chalkboards that will go in front of the items you will be serving.
- ○ A few examples for different food signs are below. You could also just write the name of the item.
  - ▶ Cool & Refreshing
  - ▶ Choose Me
  - ▶ Grab A Treat
  - ▶ Something Sweet
  - ▶ Yum
  - ▶ So Good

DAY OF:

- ○ Review the theme for today's brunch and your planned takeaways.
- ○ Decorate your event space based on your chosen summer theme.
- ○ Arrange your food items, drinks, desserts and signs.
- ○ Place a welcoming note for each lady at each place setting and welcome your guests with a refreshing drink. Lemonade, iced tea, or infused waters are great options for the summer.
- ○ Have fun!

SPOTLIGHT:

Some of the greatest gifts we have in this life come in the form of sistas, besties and friends. It's time to catch up! Try using a few icebreakers to get some conversations going.

HOW TO CHANGE IT TO A VIRTUAL EVENT:

○ Choose your virtual platform option.

○ Send a virtual invitation or email with the link/password to the brunch along with the theme of the day.

○ To maintain the lightness and sociable aspects of brunch, choose activities that create interaction with the attendees (conversation starters, ice-breakers, etc.).

○ Send activity items out prior to the event or have the attendees provide their own items/costumes/decorations. The beach trip showdown for example, can be done as a scavenger hunt with a list of items each participant has to find around their house. They have to put the items on to win.

○ Do a poll to see how many bucket list items the group has participated in.

○ Host a costume contest for the best costume that fits your theme.

Fit & Fab
Brunch
RELAX & HAVE SOME FUN

Some of the greatest gifts we have in this life come in the form of sistas, besties and friends.

SUMMER BUCKET LIST IDEAS:

- Go to a midnight movie premier
- Watch the top 10 romantic, action, thriller etc. movies of all time
- Sleep under the stars
- Have a silly string fight
- Build a blanket fort
- Take underwater pictures
- Take a road trip to somewhere new
- Plant a garden
- Have a water balloon fight
- Watch the sunrise or sunset at the beach
- Do a virtual 5k run
- Go to the spa
- Make s'mores
- Go on a hike
- Have brunch with a few friends
- Try a new restaurant
- Grow an herb garden
- Attend a virtual concert
- Make homemade ice cream
- Water tube down a river
- Spend all day at the beach
- Have a bonfire
- Drink from a coconut
- Throw a backyard cookout
- Sing your lungs out at an open mic or karaoke night

PLANNER CARE:

Okay! So you have planned out your brunch, you've sent out your invites, purchased a few snacks and decorated! 30 minutes to an hour before your party, take a few minutes to:

- ○ Freshen up

- ○ Take a breath

- ○ Pray

- ○ Sit down for a minute

- ○ Write out your goals for this event and what kind of impact you want this event to have on your group here:

ENJOY A COLD BEVERAGE AND LET'S DO BRUNCH!

LATE
NIGHT
BAKING

Travel

Garden Chronicles

DOWN BY THE BEACH

NEW ADVENTURES

Chapter 7

WELCOME BREAKFAST

Invite new members to breakfast in their honor

CHAPTER 7

WELCOME BREAKFAST

A FEW WEEKS BEFORE:

○ Choose your date and location. You can travel somewhere new or choose a group favorite.

○ Think of ways to make the new women feel special:

SOME IDEAS:

► Special invitation

► Personal phone call

► Special welcome kit, basket, or card for the new members

► Sponsor to pay for each new member's breakfast

► Send a nice invitation out to everyone. These can be paper or evites done online.

DAY OF THE EVENT:

○ Open with an Icebreaker:

SOME IDEAS:

Have each woman:

► Say one thing that may not be commonly known about them.

► Share a hobby they enjoy.

► Share what their favorite scripture is and why.

► Share something new they have recently learned or want to learn this year.

► Say one thing they enjoy about the women's group or organization.

► Choose some icebreakers from "Some Ideas to Break the Ice" in the Planning for the Year section.

- Exchange phone numbers (optional) or have everyone fill in a sign-up sheet with their contact information.

- Have fun! This is a day to get to know the new women and for them to get to know you.

- Enjoy your breakfast!

HOW TO CHANGE IT TO A VIRTUAL EVENT:

- Choose your virtual platform option.

- Send a virtual invitation or email with the link/password to the breakfast along with a picture and names of the new members that have joined in the last month, few months, or year. Personally invite the new members.

- This can be hosted as a Bring Your Own Breakfast (B.Y.O.B) event.

- Encourage everyone to wear your group SWAP (t-shirts, hats, etc.) and send some SWAG to the new members prior to the event.

- Prior to the event, have everyone sign a virtual bulletin board welcoming the new members. This can be sent to them directly after the breakfast.

- Have everyone bring something that represents them.

- Create a virtual welcome kit with your group's mission, vision, goals etc. along with a group picture and a fun roster. The fun roster would include: the name, contact information, and something fun about the person that no one else knows, a favorite hobby or their favorite breakfast item. This can be done on a virtual document that everyone can click on and fill out during the breakfast.

- If anyone in the group has a nickname, encourage them to change their name on the platform you're using to the nickname.

- ○ Create a slide deck or handout of all the group members to send out after the event with the information from the roster.

- ○ Have fun and follow up with new group members after the event.

TIPS TO HELP GROW YOUR GROUP:

It can be a little nerve-wracking joining a new group, especially if you do not really know anyone. You may wonder who you can connect with, who may share similar hobbies, or even who you can call to pray for you when you need encouragement. This is a great opportunity to get to know the other women in your group. Make a point to reach out to any new women that join in your group activities. They may want to officially join the group one day. Show your new sisters some love! Don't let the reaching out end after this event. Encourage everyone in your group to reach out to any new women whenever they see them.

SAMPLE WELCOME NOTE IDEAS

- ○ Dear (New Sister's name) we are so excited that you have joined (Group name)! Please know that we are here for you to laugh, cry, go on new adventures with, or just to talk. You are loved, important, irreplaceable, and you are welcome here!

- ○ Dear (New Sister's name) we are so happy that you are now a part of (Group name)! We are here to (list group goals/ mission) and we are here for you! We welcome and celebrate you today!

Chapter 8

BONFIRE NIGHT

A little fire + waves + good food + great company = a lot of fun

CHAPTER 8

BONFIRE NIGHT

A FEW WEEKS BEFORE

- ◯ Choose your date and location. If you are doing a backyard bonfire, exclude the beach items from your list of items to bring.

- ◯ Send a fun invitation out to everyone. These can be paper or evites done online. Include where and when you will meet up.

- ◯ Invite everyone to bring their favorite food and drink items.

SOME IDEAS TO PLAN TO BRING ARE:

- ▶ Sandals or tennis shoes depending on the time of year
- ▶ A blanket or beach chair
- ▶ Picnic cooler with ice to keep drinks and food cold
- ▶ Have everyone bring snack items to share with the group. Include items that can be cooked over the fire like: hotdogs, sausages, popcorn with different seasonings to sprinkle on it when finished, s'mores or pineapple cut into strips (caramelize over the fire by putting it on a skewer and turning the fruit every 3-5 minutes) to serve with ice cream.
- ▶ Plates, skewers, buns, toppings, condiments
- ▶ Drinks
- ▶ Wood, matches, and fire starters to start the fire or fire pit if doing a backyard bonfire
- ▶ Games
- ▶ A warm coat in case it gets chilly
- ▶ Bug repellent
- ▶ Music playlist

DAY OF THE EVENT:

○ Load up the vehicle(s) and head out to the beach.

○ Find a good spot and set up camp.

○ When building a fire, always think safety first. Be sure to clear an area and create a fire bed or ring if there is not a fire pit in place.

○ Find a great spot around the fire and have some fun!

○ Make sure to gather all trash and make sure the fire is completely out.

HOW TO CHANGE IT TO A VIRTUAL EVENT:

► Choose your virtual platform option.
► Send a virtual invitation or email with the link/password to the bonfire along with instructions on ordering a mini bonfire (if they would like).
► Turn the event into a glow in the dark bonfire by encouraging everyone to wear glow in the dark attire: necklaces, bracelets, glasses; they could even put up glow in the dark stars.
► Encourage your group to choose a fun bonfire virtual background.
► Decide on a few games that can be done virtually. These can include an icebreaker to start, a campfire tale, a devotion, or something around the theme of de-stressing. You could encourage the group to share something they do for self-care.
► Light up your campfires and make some s'mores. You can buy mini bonfires from companies like City Bonfire online. Follow the safety instructions provided.
► At this point you can wrap up the event and everyone can enjoy their bonfires.

PLANNER CARE:

Okay! So you have planned out your bonfire, you've sent out your invites, and have mapped out safe places to build a bonfire. Through the years I have found that it is hard to look out for others when you are not taking care of yourself first. I have found that a great way to de-stress from day to day is to use your creative side. Take a few minutes to color one of the coloring sheets in Appendix C.

COLORING SHEETS

► Dream Chaser
► Life to the Fullest
► Inspired

Arrange your S'mores board however you want

MOCHAS, FRAPPES & RANDOM ACTS NIGHT

Encouraging each other to encourage another

CHAPTER 9

MOCHAS, FRAPPES, AND RANDOM ACTS NIGHT

A FEW WEEKS BEFORE

○ Choose your date and location to meet. You can travel somewhere new or choose the group's favorite coffee house.

○ Send out invites to everyone in your group.

○ Encourage everyone to bring a few ideas with them.

○ Purchase a few packs of mini envelopes, decorations, and colorful paper to write on. Purchase enough for everyone to have at least three envelopes with corresponding colorful papers.

DAY OF THE EVENT:

► Arrive a little early to set up and find an area where everyone can sit.

► Arrange or scatter the envelopes, note cards, and decorative items on the tables. The note cards will be used to write down the ideas that the group comes up with.

► Meet up with everyone, purchase your drink of choice (Caramel frappé with extra caramel please!) and welcome everyone as they come over.

► Once everyone is settled, let the random acts brainstorming begin! Have someone take notes so that you can capture all the ideas. A random act can be as simple as smiling at everyone you come in contact with this week to putting together a dinner basket for new parents or buying a co-worker a thank you card for her or his help on a project. Have some fun thinking of some ideas.

○ Everyone should choose at least one random act before the night is over.

○ The choices can be used more than once if needed since everyone will be reaching out to someone different. We all interact with someone, whether it be those on our jobs, our friends and family, or with others in the places we go each day.

○ Set a date for your random acts to take place. It can take place on a certain day, span a week, or go throughout the month.

○ Have fun encouraging another through your random acts!

A FEW RANDOM ACT IDEAS:

► Call a family member you haven't seen in a while
► Put a tip in the tip jar at the coffee shop
► Let the other person have the parking space
► Don't interrupt when someone else is speaking
► Bring healthy, individually packaged treats to work for your coworkers
► Become a Big Sister
► Let the person with one or two items in the checkout line behind you go before you
► Write or visit an old teacher who made a difference in your life
► Send an e-gift card for a meal to a new mother
► Compliment someone to their boss
► Leave a nice server a nice tip

HOW TO CHANGE IT TO A VIRTUAL EVENT:

○ Choose your virtual platform option.

○ Send a virtual invitation or email with the link/password to the event.

○ Encourage everyone to either buy or make (if they have a specialty coffee maker) their favorite drink of choice prior to the start of the event.

○ Start with an icebreaker and end with an activity.

○ The host can utilize a virtual board like Trello to list the ideas or use a shared online document like a Google Doc to list the ideas from the brainstorm and who takes each idea.

○ Set a day or timeframe for the random acts to happen within.

○ Plan to meet periodically to see how it went for everyone.

SPOTLIGHT:

As the leader of your team, you are in a unique position to see everything that your team brings to the table. It is important to ensure that your team gets credit for the ideas that they share with the overall team. It is encouraging to not just feel like you are a part of the team, but that your contribution has been a part of the team's success. There is no "I" in team; however, everyone brings their abilities, strengths and ideas to make the overall team better. Recognition shown at all levels is a great way to encourage your team to continue being great.

Everyone should choose at least one random act by the end of the night.

Email or write an old teacher who made a difference in your life.

Become a big or big sister.

Compliment your boss sincerely.

Let the person with one or two items in the checkout line behind you go before you.

Bring doughnuts or a healthy treat to work

Don't interrupt when someone else is speaking.

Smile at someone you pass just because

Let the other person have the parking space.

Give someone a hug.

Call a family member

Pay the toll for the

MY SISTER'S KEEPER CHALLENGE

There may be days when we feel like the queens of the world and others when we're feeling blue. Through it all, up or down, the challenge is to look out for you. We deal with so many life issues daily. Taking care of our health including our mental health is so important. May is Mental Health Awareness Month, but you don't have to wait until then. Take the challenge to look out for your sisters, and let's encourage each other to stay healthy. Choose one or a few of the ideas below and take the time to reach out to another to show them that you care.

CHALLENGE IDEAS:

- ▶ Call a friend that you haven't spoken to in a while just to say hello.
- ▶ Send a funny joke or meme to a friend.
- ▶ Take a yoga class, go on a hike or decide on an activity of your choice with a friend.
- ▶ Don't force your help on them. Offer your help but if they decline, accept that.
- ▶ Meet up with a friend for mochas and make a to-do-list together. Help her accomplish one item.
- ▶ Be someone they can trust. Don't share with others what was shared with you in confidence.
- ▶ Plan a Girl's Night Out and have some fun.
- ▶ Bake something homemade and take it to a friend.
- ▶ Genuinely ask how a friend is doing and simply listen offering emotional support.
- ▶ Hang out with a friend for the day.

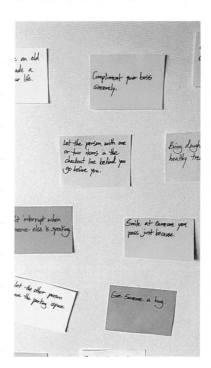

- Let them know that you are there for them.
- Send a framed picture you took with a friend to them with a nice note or card.
- Take a sister out to lunch, or go on a movie date.
- Don't assume you know what is best for them.
- Put a care package together for a friend in need.
- Check out mentalhealthamerica. net to conduct awareness activities for Mental Health Awareness Month in May.

MAXIMUM CAPACITY – BY JAMILA KAMARIA BROWN

Many days had been spent living life at maximum capacity

Rushing here or there

Needing to do this or that

Expectations, deadlines, one more thing...added into my already

overwhelmed but highly decorated planner spread.

How can I encourage myself

Keep myself uplifted

Motivate myself to follow my dreams

In the midst of all

of this?

I need my sisters and sister friends,

My Frappé with extra caramel,

My let's go hang out,

Do something fun,

Get our minds off this hustle,

type of friends to keep me grounded.

To help me remember that I was made for more

and that this is not it!

So laugh a little, cry a little if you have to.

And tomorrow, I'm going to need you to

Stop and smell the roses,

Run barefoot down the beach and into the waves,

Laugh and laugh until our sides hurt,

And know that you can do this

if only one day

at a time.

IN THE MIDST OF IT ALL, AND ON DAYS WHEN YOU NEED A REMINDER IN CASE YOU FORGOT... YOU ARE FEARFULLY & WONDERFULLY MADE!

Chapter 10

IN CELEBRATION OF YOU, MAMA

For Mother's Day

CHAPTER 10

IN CELEBRATION OF YOU, MAMA
- FOR MOTHER'S DAY

Many have fond memories of foods their mom cooked for them as children. What better way to preserve these memories than to put them together into a cookbook! Living, building, breathing, and remembering the legacy of those that came before us. This can be an individual activity or as a group you can put together a book and have copies made for all the participants and their mom or mother figure.

A FEW MONTHS PRIOR:

○ Gather recipes: These can either be your favorite recipes from your mom, or ones that you hold dear to your heart from your grandmother, aunt, godmother, sister or mother figure to you.

○ Type out the recipes and either bind them professionally or print and bind them yourself with ribbon and binder rings; place in a binder or use some other type of binding materials. Before binding, you can add in fond memories of time spent with her, add a letter to her, or add a few poems. You can even bullet journal ways that you appreciate her on a page of your book. Why are these recipes so memorable? Are there any stories behind the food that you would like to include?

○ If your mother is no longer living, you may want to do a tribute to her on a page of your book. Include some things that you want to remember about her, and some lessons learned. Maybe she had some sayings that she quoted often, these can be included as well.

○ Make as many copies of the book as needed.

ON MOTHER'S DAY:

○ In the United States, Mother's Day is celebrated on the second Sunday of May (Taken from timeanddate.com). This day can vary depending on where you are in the world. If your country doesn't have a formal day of recognition you can still celebrate on the day of your choosing.

○ Wrap and present to your mom or mother figure.

○ Invite them either out to lunch or dinner, or to a home-cooked dinner.

○ If your mother is no longer living, do something to honor your mom. Celebrate the day by doing something she liked to do and eating some of her favorite foods.

○ **Note:** This can also be done as a Celebration of Dad on Father's Day celebrated on the third Sunday of June in the United States (Taken from timeanddate.com) or whatever day you choose.

JAMILA'S SALMON RUB

Preheat oven to 450 degrees Fahrenheit.

INGREDIENTS:

½ cup dark brown sugar, 1 tbsp. low sodium soy sauce, juice from ½ fresh lemon, 1 tsp. ground black pepper, ½ tsp. salt, ½ tsp. garlic powder, 2 tsp. onion powder, 3 tsp. dry parsley, ¼ tsp. ground cayenne red pepper, ¼ tsp. celery salt, 2.5 lb. salmon fillet.

DIRECTIONS:

Rinse fish well under cool water and pat dry. Mix together dry ingredients first with the brown sugar, and then add in wet ingredients. Mix well and gently rub into fish all over. Bake for 4 to 6 minutes per ½- inch thickness. Fish is done once it flakes easily. Do not overcook it. Enjoy!

SERVE WITH:

Your favorite side dishes and dessert.

I've served a variety of side dishes with it through the years including:

- ▶ Garlic mashed potatoes
- ▶ Tossed green salad with a variety of veggies and a nice dressing
- ▶ Roasted oven potatoes (either seasoned, diced Yukon's or seasoned baby potatoes)
- ▶ Mini Pommes Anna

SPOTLIGHT:

Take some time out to honor the legacy of those that came before you. Their passions, their dreams, their hopes, their history, their legacy. Paving the way for future generations, we look to them and have looked to them for wisdom, a listening ear, advice on life, or a treasured recipe. Growing up I loved my mom's meatloaf, cabbage, made-from-scratch cornbread, and giant oatmeal cookies. Never forget those who came before us, because of them we are! Today let's celebrate Mama, Mom, Mother, Ma, Madré, Mum, Nana, Grandma, Grams, Auntie, Tía, Sister, Sissy, God Mom, and friend!

"A people without knowledge of its past is like a tree without roots."

Marcus Garvey

Chapter 11

A GEM LIKE NO OTHER

We value gems and precious stones but you are so much more precious than these

CHAPTER 11

"A GEM LIKE NO OTHER"
- WOMEN'S WORKSHOP

We value gems and precious stones, but as women we are much more precious than these. We are worth so much more!

"Surely they may forget, Yet I will not forget you. See, I have inscribed you on the palms of My hands; Your walls are continually before Me."

Isaiah 49:15b-16 NKJV

A FEW MONTHS OUT:

- Mark your calendar for the date that works best for your group.

- Reserve your venue.

- Choose your workshop facilitator and send them a nice invitation with the date, theme, and any other important information they should know.

- Fun fact: March is National Women's History Month!

- Search the internet for fun facts about women throughout history. Don't limit your search as women have contributed to many different areas. You can also choose a woman that is making strides her own way who may not be famous yet. Put these fun facts and pictures of the women up on a board, around the venue in nice picture frames, or up on the wall with different patterned background papers in the theme color.

THESE ARE A FEW OF MY FAVORITES:

▶ **Misty Copeland:** The first African American Female Principal Dancer with the prestigious American Ballet Theater. Her story is so inspiring and shows that you can still go after your dreams despite all the odds.

▶ **Florence Delorez Griffith Joyner (Flo Jo):** Considered the fastest woman of all time. Growing up I loved to watch the sprinters in the Summer Olympics. Watching Flo Jo run the 100 meter, 200 meter and 4x100 was so amazing!

▶ **Edna Lewis:** An African American chef and author best known for her books on traditional Southern cuisine. She received the Lifetime Achievement Award from the International Association of Culinary Professionals and is lauded as one of the great women of American cooking. She received the James Beard Living Legend Award, their first such award in 1999.

○ Invite vendors that cater to your group's interests to showcase their products and services.

○ Purchase a few large faux precious stones (e.g. like a large diamond or ruby) from an arts and crafts store or online.

○ Send a fun invite out to everyone in your group and beyond. Include the theme, "A G.E.M. (Gorgeous, Encouraged, and Marvelous) Like No Other."

○ Encourage everyone to bring a picture of a woman they admire to post on a large board or marked off section of a wall during the event. This will be a backdrop for a group photo at the end of the event. Have the words "We are fearfully & wonderfully made," above the pictures. Plan ahead to have some pictures available in case someone forgot to bring their picture with them. You could also frame out the designated space with the preselected photos to have a more complete wall of pictures.

DAY OF CELEBRATION:

- ○ Set the scene for the skit. See "Setting the scene" below.

- ○ Introduce your skit.

- ○ Skit time.

"In Case You Forgot...You Are Fearfully & Wonderfully Made"

An Interactive Skit

Working to change negative messages to positive messages.

Messages about body shaming, bullying, and insecurities about body image can be seen everywhere around us and in the news. Due to a growing awareness of these issues, we hear stories of people who have been body shamed or bullied and we also see people taking a stand against it. We come in so many different sizes and shapes and no one is an exact copy of anyone. Sometimes it can be easy to get caught up in the "I wish I looked like her," or the "If I could change this about myself," thoughts. Yes, I've been guilty of it too. But we have to remember that God created us all differently, no one is exactly the same in this world. In case you forgot...You are fearfully & wonderfully made!

GOALS OF SKIT:

○ To work towards not focusing on negative outside opinions, negative internal opinions and instead replace them with positive ones.

○ To review some common stereotypes related to body shaming and outside perceptions.

○ Discussion around these negative outside/inside opinions.

○ To bring awareness to the risk factors and effects of bullying. See stopbullying.gov for some of these.

○ To encourage everyone to speak life, health, and positive body image in place of negative outside/inside opinions.

○ For everyone to realize that we are more than just a perception. Who we are is more than skin deep. What makes us tick, the dreams and goals we have for our lives, our favorites, our beliefs, or where we want to travel one day; these are what make us who we are. Relish these, protect these, live these.

SETTING THE SCENE:

○ Around the room, post a few statistics regarding eating disorders, cutting, and other actions some have taken because they feel less than.

○ Pass out a handout with some information on bullying:

○ Some items you may want to include are (taken from stopbullying. gov):

► The two modes of bullying include direct (e.g. bullying that occurs in the presence of a targeted youth) and indirect (e.g. bullying not directly communicated to a targeted youth such as spreading rumors).

ACT 1

Group of friends out shopping: Enter from the back of the venue laughing and talking about a favorite TV show. Upon arrival at the front of the audience start looking through the rack of women's clothing.

First friend: Do you guys think this would look good on me? Takes a pair of pants off the rack and holds it against her body.

Second friend: Uh...I think they would be a little tight.

Third friend: Girl, with those thick thighs you'd be lucky to get one leg in.

First friend: Puts the pants back on the rack. She continues to look through the rack of clothes a little less joyfully.

Group of friends: Exits out a side door heading to the next store. The second and third friend laughing about another TV show. They are oblivious of how deeply their words have affected their friend.

Stage crew: Move clothing rack to the side of stage.

ACT 2

Outside influences: (a few women depending on how many body shaming terms you will use) Dressed in all black, enter from the back of the venue carrying white poster boards placing them on the easels in the front of the audience. Write a commonly heard or seen body shaming term in large letters on each white poster board in black ink.

Some examples of common body shaming terms/phrases are:

- Pooch
- Muffin or cupcake top
- Saddlebags
- Thunder thighs
- Curvaceous
- You're pretty for a….
- I feel so fat
- Do I look fat?
- Love handles
- Double chin or old faithful
- Spare tire
- Cankles
- Tall for a girl
- Eat a sandwich
- Man hands
- Sausage fingers
- Bigfoot
- Boats
- Cultural attributes (varies depending on culture)

ACT 3

First Friend: Back from shopping, she is shown in her bedroom crying.

Sister of First Friend: Enters first friend's bedroom telling her that dinner is ready. Noticing that she was crying, asks if she is okay.

First Friend: Quickly wiping her tears away, tells her she is fine.

Sister of First Friend: Says okay and exits bedroom.

First Friend: Goes down for dinner, but shortly after is seen in the bathroom throwing up her dinner. Unrecognized by her family this has become a common theme. She returns to her bedroom to lie down.

End of scene

GROUP INTERACTION

○ Have the friends and outside influences come back in to facilitate.

○ Open the floor for discussion on the following:

BODY SHAMING DISCUSSION:

▶ Ask if they have ever heard any common body shaming terms used in reference to themselves or have used these in reference to someone else.

▶ Ask how they felt when these terms were used to describe them and the effect it had on the other person.

▶ We will next look at internal influences.

INTERNAL INFLUENCES DISCUSSION:

○ Have everyone describe themselves in three words. This can include one thing they feel defines them, a description of their outer appearance etc.

▶ Have the facilitators gather and read the three words aloud.

▶ Address any negative internal influences.

○ When did they start feeling this way about themselves?

○ Did someone else tell them this about themselves?

○ Have they taken any action that would be harmful to themselves? Have a professional there that can address these and where they can get help. If a professional is not available, have resource information available for them to take with them.

○ Pass out a white sticky note and a colorful sticky note to the group.

- ▶ Next have them write down one thing they secretly or do not secretly dislike about themselves on the white sticky note.
- ▶ When done, have them crumble this sticky note up and dispose of it in buckets that the facilitators will take around.
- ○ Turn around the poster boards that were used earlier to the blank side. On the top of each write: "I am"

"I AM" DISCUSSION:

- ○ Have everyone write on their colorful sticky note one of the following:
  - ▶ Something they love about themselves.
  - ▶ One thing they wish others knew about them.
  - ▶ One of the positive terms below:

Awesome, Creative, Smart, Classy, Talented, Beautiful, Fearless, Queen, or another word that describes how fabulous they truly are.

  - ▶ Have everyone share what they have written (if they feel comfortable sharing) and post their colorful sticky note on the white poster boards in the front.

- ○ End the skit with one of the facilitators reading the "In Case You Forgot" poem or another poem that celebrates being fearfully and wonderfully made.

I LOVE THIS ABOUT MYSELF

WRITE ONE THING YOU WISH OTHERS KNEW ABOUT YOU

WHO AM I?

DESCRIBE YOURSELF IN THREE WORDS

A GEM LIKE NO OTHER
INTERACTIVE ACTIVIT

IN CASE YOU FORGOT – BY JAMILA KAMARIA BROWN

In case you ever forget

When life's cares seem too heavy to bear

When the busyness of the day to day starts to set in.

Taking care of family, working hard on the 9 to 5,

commuting through days, and evenings, and nights.

Paying bills, cooking meals, taking care of house and home.

Fixing vehicles, striving to follow dreams and the disposition of your heart.

In the midst of it all,

In case you forgot...you are fearfully & wonderfully made!

In case no one ever told you,

In case you seek positivity but it eludes you,

In case you sometimes feel so low that you struggle to survive.

In case you forget in the midst of it all that you

are loved.

There is now no one like you,

and there will never be again.

You were formed in your mother's womb

one of a kind, unique.

All of your parts, created to be a masterpiece.

Let go of what others think

when they try to project their own insecurities

of body image upon you.

Who gave them the power to define who you are?

Who made them God?

God said who we would be before we were a

whisper in the wind.

Such dreams, such passion...

She will be one of my greatest creations.

In case you forgot, you are fearfully & wonderfully made!

Psalm 139:13-14 NKJV says, "For You formed my inward parts; You covered me in my mother's womb.

I will praise You, for I am fearfully and wonderfully made; Marvelous

are Your works, And that my soul knows very well."

Some will lie, bold faced because of their own insecurities.

Some will do so because they feel threatened.

Do you, my friend, because in the end

they can't change who you are unless you give them the power.

They can't determine the course of your life, only you can.

Their realities and thoughts will only determine their own course.

Reject the projected insecurities, and negativity

They have no power to control your destiny.

Live your life your way, unapologetically.

In the midst of it all, and on days when you need a reminder

In case you forgot...You are fearfully & wonderfully made!

AFFIRMATION CEREMONY:

We spend a lot of time taking care of the outside, our appearance, our makeup, our clothes, but it is also important to uplift and encourage other women and to focus on the inner woman. We go through so much and deal with so much every day. An encouraging word may be just what is needed to lift someone's spirit, motivate them to press on, or give them the strength to do what they need to do.

Have everyone line up in two lines facing each other:

○ Everyone will go down the line receiving affirmations from those on each side. For example:

  ► You were designed for greatness
  ► You are whole and complete
  ► You are loved
  ► You are irreplaceable
  ► You are in this place and in this space for a reason
  ► You are somebody's sunshine
  ► I believe in you and your ability to succeed
  ► You have resources to handle anything that comes into your life, etc.

○ This is an opportunity to say an encouraging word, show appreciation, pray for, or uplift each woman in the group as they go down the line. Have some tissues available since this can be a very emotional activity.

○ You can have the women close their eyes as they go down the line.

Have special treats/refreshments for everyone afterwards.

○ This will be a time to mingle with the vendors and other women at the event.

○ Create a G.E.M. tote bag for everyone.

  ► This can be a tote bag printed with the workshop theme/title filled with treats, business cards or an overall list of the vendors, quotes on nice paper, a special prayer, faux gem, notebook, snack item, jewelry item, water bottle etc.

HOW TO CHANGE IT TO A VIRTUAL EVENT:

○ Choose your virtual platform option.

○ Send a virtual invitation or email with the link/password to the webinar, along with the date, theme, and any important information attendees should know.

○ A tote bag with event supplies can be distributed prior to the webinar.

○ Choose someone prior to the event to read the "In Case You Forgot" poem.

○ Encourage the attendees to post a woman they admire as their virtual background. Allow time for them to say why they chose their woman.

○ The skit can be prerecorded and played through the host's computer - see Setting the scene for the skit details.

▶ After the skit, open the webinar up for discussion - see Group Interaction.

▶ Instead of the facilitator gathering group responses, either the group can share them aloud or you could create polls with specific questions through websites like Mentimeter where the host would display the word cloud by sharing their screen. As the group posts their answers to the question, the word cloud would grow.

QUESTIONS CAN INCLUDE:

- ▶ Describe yourself in three words...
- ▶ I am... with the group filling in the blank. See "I am" section for ideas
- ▶ Who am I...?
- ▶ I love this about myself...
- ▶ One thing you wish others knew about you...
- ▶ You can have the group write down more personal responses with the option to share or not.

○ Everyone can prepare their own treats in advance or include non-perishable packaged snacks inside their tote bags.

○ Vendors selling goods and services that cater to your group can be done through breakout rooms.

Give participants the option to choose their breakout rooms and they can go back and forth between the vendors during a set time.

Encourage the vendors to share their purchasing information, website, and/or product list ahead of time in the workshop materials or add their webpage/link information to their virtual background within their breakout room.

VIRTUAL AFFIRMATION CEREMONY:

○ This will work similar to an in-person affirmation line except during each person's turn, you may be able to pin their name within the virtual platform so that their picture stays up during their affirmations and have everyone take their turn.

○ Have a list of attendees to share with the group prior to the start, and go down the list of names sharing affirmations.

PLANNER CARE:

Okay! So you have planned out your workshop, you've sent out your invites, decorated the venue and you are waiting for everyone to arrive. 30 minutes to an hour before your start time, take a few minutes to:

- ○ Freshen up

- ○ Take a breath

- ○ Pray

- ○ Sit down for a minute

- ○ Think of a few things that make you uniquely you and how these things have helped you grow as a leader. Keep these in mind as you encourage everyone that attends today's event. After all, you are a gem as well!

- ○ Write them out here:

IN CASE YOU FORGOT, YOU ARE FEARFULLY AND WONDERFULLY MADE.

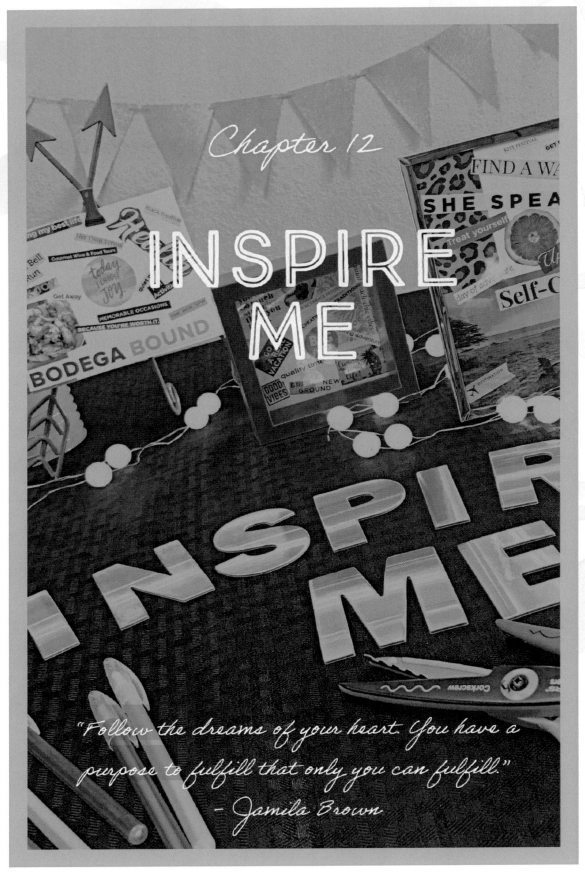

Chapter 12

INSPIRE ME

"Follow the dreams of your heart. You have a purpose to fulfill that only you can fulfill."
— Jamila Brown

CHAPTER 12

"INSPIRE ME"

VISION & GOALS POP-UP

What is it that makes you come alive, what makes you unique, what do you bring to the table? We all have something to contribute to this world, we all have a part to play, but many give up before they even realize their full potential. Don't give into the cookie cutter mentality; there is no one else like you and no one can do you or the things you do like you. Come be inspired to walk your walk unapologetically. We are not here to compete; we are here to do what God has given us to do. No one else has your vision, your purpose, and your talents. Inspire the world and just do you!

A FEW MONTHS PRIOR:

- ○ **Set your pop-up date and time.** Reserve a nice location in a fun city. It would be helpful to book a location that includes smaller breakout rooms that can be available for the mini sessions.

- ○ **Send out invites** that will encourage, inspire, or get women thinking about purpose (See example invitation).

INVITATION IDEA:

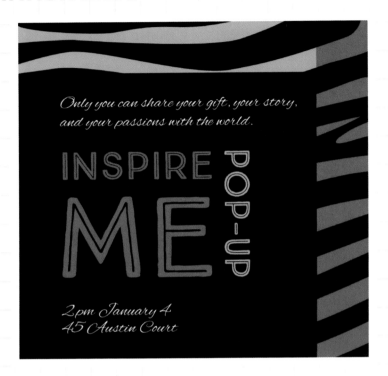

Only you can share your gift, your story, and your passions with the world.

INSPIRE ME POP-UP

2pm January 4
45 Austin Court

- ○ **Invite a few speakers** from a variety of fields (For example: Law, Medical, Culinary Arts, Business, Art & Design, Undecided – Life coach) and one well rounded main speaker. The mini session speakers will inspire their groups to pursue their dreams in their field of choice; the overall speaker will speak to all groups.

- ○ **Invite a few vendors:** Jewelry, makeup, fashion, caterer or other vendors that would be a fit for your group.

- ○ **Purchase any supplies needed for the workshop:** Folders, name badges, decorative paper & cards to write on, and other vision board lounge supplies.

DAY OF EVENT:

- ○ **Have everyone register.** At the registration table they can sign-in, take a name badge, and folder with workshop materials, and write on a My Gifts and Passions postcard (see Appendix D for a template idea that can be printed prior to the event or you can create your own version) what they feel their gifts or passions in life are (this can be something they are good at or enjoy doing, a hobby, etc.). Have them write their mailing address on the backside of the card. These will be mailed out to everyone after the workshop. Post these on the wall during the Pop-up. Next, have everyone take a 5-minute questionnaire (you can create your own or find one online) about their interests/goals that will determine the mini session they will go to. Play soft music or music appropriate for your group in the background.

- ○ **Introduce the vision board lounge:** This will be a purposeful space for everyone to create their vision for their life, work, family, dreams, or goals.

- ▶ Prior to your event collect all kinds of magazines that can be cut up.
- ▶ On the day of the event, arrange the vision board lounge items in a specific area of your venue that can be visited throughout the event. Some items to have available: cardstock, glue sticks, magazines, colorful pens or markers, stamps, ribbon, scrapbooking paper, scrapbooking scissors, regular scissors, inspirational quotes, sticky notes, stickers, and nice signs that explain the purpose of a vision board. Have everyone take a photo of their vision board so they will not only have a hard copy but an electronic copy of their board.
- ▶ As everyone visits the vision board lounge, they will be given a vision board background (this can be a piece of colorful or white cardstock, a map, etc.) and will be able to cut out words, pictures, and quotes from the magazines that represent what their vision, goals, and dreams for their life are for this year and beyond. They can also write words with markers or an ink pen.

○ **Place a few signs around the vision board lounge to get everyone started.**

Here are a few ideas:

▶ Release the power behind your goals by making them visible.
▶ Keep your goals at the forefront of your mind. Post them somewhere visible where you can see them daily.
▶ Continue to work towards your dreams.
▶ Where have you always wanted to travel? What financial goals do you want to reach? If you could do one thing and money was not an issue what would it be?

○ **Break into groups:**

▶ Mini session time. Get inspired by one of the mini session leaders!
▶ Next, within the small groups, have everyone think about their own purpose or passion in life. Have them brainstorm 3 things they can do to use this purpose or passion in their everyday life. Have each group share theirs (if they like) in their small groups. This time can also be used to help everyone brainstorm how they can use their purpose or passion.

○ **Have a Mini Snack Break:**

▶ Everyone can visit the vendors and enjoy some light refreshments and tasty snacks.

○ You may want to consider having different assessment tests available:

▶ Like a personality assessment or spiritual gift test.

○ End the day with a group picture or group selfie:

▶ Have everyone hold up their vision board.

EVENT TAKEAWAY IDEAS:

► You were born with a purpose, find it, pursue it, and be encouraged!

► Someone may be in need of your gift. Only you can share your gift, your story, and your passions with the world.

► No one else can do you, so be who you were created to be, and don't look back.

► To be encouraged to work on your goals and dreams every day. They will only come to be if you actively pursue them.

► To not discount or downplay your gifts in the midst of others' insecurities. You have an obligation to do, live and be your best every day.

► To not be discouraged by whatever your situation may be. You are awesome, and you are here for a reason. You have one life to live, one or many purposes to fulfill, and only you can do it like you!

► You have the ability to change things about your life. Focus on doing something each day to take yourself closer to where you would like to be, even if just for thirty minutes a day.

FOR QUOTE BACKGROUND, CHOOSE A FEW BELOW OR FIND A FEW OF YOUR OWN.

"Be You. The world will adjust."

– Author unknown

"If you don't understand yourself you don't understand anybody else."

– Nikki Giovanni

"You're not obligated to win. You're obligated to keep trying to do the best you can every day."

– Marian Wright Edelman

"Every great dream begins with a dreamer. Always remember, you have within you the strength, the patience, and the passion to reach for the stars to change the world."

– Harriet Tubman

"I have learned over the years that when one's mind is made up, this diminishes fear; knowing what must be done does away with fear."

– Rosa Parks

"No person has the right to rain on your dreams."

– Marian Wright Edelman

"It isn't where you come from; it's where you're going that counts."

– Ella Fitzgerald

"Never be limited by other people's limited imaginations."

– Dr. Mae Jemison

"One of the lessons that I grew up with was to always stay true to yourself and never let what somebody else says distract you from your goals. And so when I hear about negative and false attacks, I really don't invest any energy in them, because I know who I am."

– Michelle Obama

"Amidst all of the uncertainty of this season, something beautiful is growing here, and one day you will look back and see that all along, all by grace, you were blooming."

– Morgan Harper Nichols

"We are all gifted. That is our inheritance."

– Ethel Waters

"Never underestimate the power of dreams and the influence of the human spirit. We are all the same in this notion: The potential for greatness lives within each of us."

– Wilma Rudolph

"Just like moons and like suns, with the certainty of tides. Just like hopes springing high, Still I'll rise."

– Maya Angelou

"You are loved more than you will ever know."

– Author unknown

"Remember that I have commanded you to be determined and confident! Do not be afraid or discouraged, for I, the Lord your God, am with you wherever you go."

– Joshua 1:9 GNT

"Great heights reached and kept by men were not attained through sudden flights, but those men, while their friends were sleeping, toiled through the night."

– Mpule Kwelagobe

"I've come a long way from being the girl who thought she wasn't good enough."

– grindpretty.com

"Rise up, sis. you have a purpose, even now."

– @hertrueworth

"Follow the dreams of your heart. You have a purpose that only you can fulfill. You have a dream to share that only you can share."

– Jamila Kamaria Brown

"Everything you take for granted, that comes natural to you, is a gift connected to a calling. We all have one. No more playing small."

– Bete Agonafer

HOW TO CHANGE IT TO A VIRTUAL EVENT:

○ Choose your virtual platform option.

○ Send a virtual invitation or email with the link/password to the Pop-up, along with the details of what supplies to bring for their vision board, and a link to an online survey to collect specific information from the group. This preregistration can be done through Google Forms.

○ Event quotes, activities, and materials can be provided in advance to the attendees.

○ You can use breakout rooms for your speakers.

  ► Give attendees the option to choose their breakout room.
  ► Set a timer for the breakout room so attendees can swap between breakout rooms to hear different speakers during the event. The amount of time is up to you but allow at least 10 to 15 minutes per speaker.

○ Before sending everyone to the breakout rooms, introduce the vision board lounge.

  ► Have someone host this breakout room and play relaxing music through their computer.
  ► Participants will provide their own supplies for their vision board.
  ► This breakout room can have a few presentation slides with tips on creating a vision board.

SPOTLIGHT:

In a group, it is important to value and respect everyone's gifts, talents, and skills equally, regardless of their role in the group. Every contribution is valuable and adds life to the group. The soft-spoken cheerleader in the back row is just as vital as the charismatic speaker upfront. Utilize everyone's strengths, gifts, talents, and skills, and look for opportunities to do so.

ONLY YOU
CAN SHARE
YOUR GIFT,
YOUR STORY,
AND YOUR
PASSIONS
WITH THE
WORLD.

DON'T LEAVE YOUR PLANS TO OTHERS TO CARRY OUT, IT'S YOUR VISION, YOUR DREAM TO FULFILL.

– JAMILA K. BROWN

PLANNER CARE:

Okay! So you have planned out your Vision Board & Goals Pop-up, you've sent out your invites, decorated the venue and you are waiting for everyone to arrive. 30 minutes to an hour before your start time, take a few minutes to:

○ Freshen up

○ Take a breath

○ Pray

○ Sit down for a minute

○ Think of how you are sharing your gifts with the world. Are you living up to your full potential? Think of one or two ways to step out and follow your dreams. Let go of the fear, discouragement or doubt. God placed that dream in your heart for a reason; it is yours, so step out and live it.

WRITE THEM OUT HERE:

WE WORK TOWARD THE VISION WE HAVE SEEN IN OUR HEARTS. EVERY PHONE CALL, EVERY DETAIL, EVERY STEP OF THE WAY IS A PIECE OF THE MASTERPIECE.
– JAMILA K. BROWN

Chapter 13

HOLIDAY CELEBRATION

The end of the year is often a time of reflection. Gather a few friends and have some fun wrapping up the year!

HOLIDAY CELEBRATION

A FEW WEEKS TO A MONTH OUT:

- ○ Choose your date.

- ○ Choose a special theme of the day. This would include decorations, special drinks, games, etc. For the events that are not based around food, you can have some snacks ready to go (see pre-made snack ideas below).

HERE ARE A FEW IDEAS:

- ○ **Holidays around the World:** Everyone brings a holiday dish and holiday tradition to share from a different part of the world.

- ○ **Christmas Cookie Exchange:** The group will all bring two dozen homemade Christmas cookies to share, and everyone will leave with two dozen cookies.

- ○ **Ugly Sweater, Ugly Socks or Ugly Robes Night:** Why stop at ugly sweaters or ugly socks. Everyone can choose their own ugly item to wear, or you can choose one of the items. Imagine creating the ultimate ugly robe that will top all others. The sole purpose of this theme is to have fun!

- **Christmas Past, Present, and Future:** Caroling for Christmas past, White Elephant for Christmas present and collecting small gifts to donate to a children's group or home for Christmas future. You could also create your own mix of activities. For example: Baking your favorite holiday cookies for Christmas past, Collecting donations for a local homeless shelter for Christmas present and Writing a holiday letter to your future self or to your child with favorite memories and recipes.

- **Winter Wonderland – A formal affair:** Everyone gets dressed up for an evening of fun.

- **Holiday PJs:** Wear your best holiday PJs for an evening of fun. Host a PJ contest with several categories such as "most comfy," or "most holiday spirit."

- **12 Days of Christmas:** This theme is a play on the "12 Days of Christmas" song; however, you will create your own modern version representing 12 must do items/activities that must be done before Christmas. They will be represented in the activities, songs, or food items for the day. Break the group in teams, and in their invite notify them of what item/activity they will represent. They will need to bring something representing this on the day of the event.

- **Balance, Beauty & Batter:** This will be a holiday pancake breakfast where balance and beauty are the topics of the day as you enjoy a pancake bar with many different toppings and sides. Provide drinks like OJ, coffee, and water.

- **Bring Your Own Biscuits (B.Y.O.B.):** This version of the balance & beauty day includes a holiday brunch where everyone brings their favorite holiday brunch item to share along with their favorite beauty tip. Have everyone write their tip on a colorful card and post it on the wall or easel with a poster board. Include a short discussion on the importance of finding your balance in life. Provide fun holiday drinks like hot chocolate, a coffee bar with peppermint stick stirrers, or eggnog.

- **Brains, Beauty & Beignets:** This day will be a holiday game-themed brunch where beignets, doughnuts or other pastries will be the main food items. Provide drinks like OJ, coffee, and water. Have everyone wear their favorite holiday outfit for a group selfie. Plan out a few holiday games and let the competition begin!

- Send out cute invites. These can be paper versions or an online version (see invite example). Let everyone know beforehand what the theme of the day will be and what to bring. Include details like what to wear if it is a dress up party or PJ party for example.

Sample holiday menu brought to you by Chef Afiya Griffith:

For this event we are keeping it festive and fun!

- ▶ Build Your Own Pancake Bar (Toppings: Choc Chips, blueberries, cinnamon apple, confetti)
- ▶ Roasted Red Pepper & Caramelized Red Onion Scramble
- ▶ Glazed Cranberry and Blood Orange Muffins
- ▶ Smoked Chorizo Hash
- ▶ Fruit & Roasted Chestnut Parfait
- ▶ Honey & Spice Basted Ham

INVITATION IDEA:

1st Holiday Pancake Breakfast

BALANCE, BEAUTY & BATTER
DEC 3

4pm at 230 Lovewell Court

WEEK OF CELEBRATION:

○ Purchase or buy supplies to make a few pre-made snacks or dishes:

Depending on the theme of your party, you may want to have a few snack items available for your group. Some Ideas: Deviled eggs, mini sandwiches, pre-made appetizers that you bake, and some drinks like punch, coffee, and water are good to have on hand. You could also have a hot beverage bar that includes hot milk for hot chocolate, or hot water for tea.

DAY OF CELEBRATION:

○ Mix and mingle.

○ Depending on your theme choice, carry out your plan for the day.

○ Have fun and take lots of pictures to add to your group scrapbook.

REFLECTION ACTIVITY:

Have these questions typed out on a handout for everyone. Give them a few minutes to write down their responses to the following:

- ► What is one thing you have learned this year and how will you use it going forward?
- ► Why did this thing impact your life?
- ► What goal(s) did you set for yourself this year? Were you able to reach them?
- ► What did you enjoy most this year?
- ► What are your new goals for the year? Encourage them to set some dates for these items later on.

RECIPE FOR A HOLIDAY PLATTER

INGREDIENTS:

- ► Platter – Be creative with the color or shape of the platter
- ► Veggies, fruit, desserts, or appetizers
- ► Serving dishes for any dips
- ► Serving utensils if needed

DIRECTIONS:

- ► **Step 1:** Okay, first decide what type of platter you want to create – whether a veggie, fruit, dessert, or appetizer platter.
- ► **Step 2:** Use favorite recipes, find recipes online, or purchase items to fill your platter.
- ► **Step 3:** Arrange the items nicely or lay them out in a pattern. For example, if you are doing a dessert platter, you could lay out so many of one cookie then start another row of another type of cookie. Keep alternating the cookies and types of cookies until your platter is full. If you are doing a veggie platter you could put the dishes holding the veggie dip in the center and surround those dishes with so many of one veggie, then another until the platter is full. Have fun, it's your platter, you make the rules.

STEWED CHICKEN – BY CHEF AFIYA GRIFFITH

INGREDIENTS:

6 pieces of chicken (legs or thighs), 1 onion, 1 red bell pepper, 6 cloves garlic, 1 scotch bonnet pepper (please take care and use gloves when handling hot peppers), Grace hot pepper sauce, Maggie or Goya chicken bouillon, tomato paste, salt, pepper, garlic and onion powder, allspice, thyme, white vinegar, 1 red potato. Chicken bath: Limes, Vinegar, Salt.

DIRECTIONS:

Place chicken in a bowl. Pour enough water to cover, and add half a cup of vinegar and the juice squeezed from 3 limes. This solution will help clean the chicken and remove impurities. After the chicken has sat in the solution for about 20 minutes, rub and rinse the chicken. Now poke holes in chicken with a fork or knife and sprinkle with a little allspice, salt, thyme, garlic powder, onion powder and cracked pepper. Meanwhile, dice 1 red pepper, ¾ of an onion, ½ of a scotch bonnet pepper (please wear gloves when dicing and touching the pepper and discard them before touching anything else), and 6 cloves of garlic. In a deep pot pour enough oil to coat the bottom. Bring to medium-high heat, place chicken in pot to sear on both sides. Once seared remove from pot and reduce heat to medium heat. Add chopped vegetables, cook until translucent. Season vegetables with salt and pepper. Stir and add ¾ small can of tomato paste, stir for one minute then add 6-7 cups of water. Bring to a simmer, add more seasoning if needed (fresh veggies or spices from earlier). Now add chicken, stir and leave uncovered.

Add 3 chicken bouillon (Goya or Maggie), a couple of shakes (5) of Grace hot pepper sauce, and a ¼ cup of white vinegar. Stir once again and continue to watch pot until juices have reduced. Add water at this point, chicken should be submerged and covered in juice. Stir and let reduce until the chicken begins to fall off the bone and the juice has naturally thickened; at this point add one red diced potato. Let cook until potatoes are tender. Turn off heat, serve over rice.

RICE FOR STEWED CHICKEN:

INGREDIENTS:

1 ½ cup water, ½ juice from chicken pot, 1 bag of red sazon seasoning, 1 teaspoon salt, 1 cup rice.

DIRECTIONS:

Add liquids to pot and seasonings. Bring to a boil, add rice and stir. Cover and cook over medium-low heat for about 15 minutes until rice is fluffy and tender.

1st Holiday Pancake Breakfast

BALANCE, BEAUTY & BATTER

LIFE IS SHORT, MAKE IT SWEET!

HOW TO CHANGE IT TO A VIRTUAL EVENT:

○ Choose your virtual platform option.

○ Choose a theme that will work well on a virtual platform like:

► Ugly Sweater, Ugly Socks or Ugly Robes Night
► Brains, Beauty & Beignets
► Bring Your Own Biscuits (B.Y.O.B)
► Winter Wonderland

○ Send a virtual invitation or email with the link/password to the webinar, along with the date, theme and any other important information attendees should know.

○ Encourage attendees to participate in the theme through decorating, dressing up, or sending out a virtual background that represents the theme.

○ Plan out activities based on your theme.

○ The host can play holiday music through their computer and the virtual platform.

○ Attendees can provide their own snacks based on the theme.

○ Have a contest with the "best decorated" or "best dressed."

○ Take snapshots throughout the event.

○ End with the Reflection activity.

PLANNER CARE:

Okay! So you have planned out your celebration, you've put together your holiday platter, decorated the venue and you are waiting for everyone to arrive. 30 minutes to an hour before your start time, take a few minutes to:

- ○ Freshen up

- ○ Take a breath

- ○ Pray

- ○ Sit down for a minute

- ○ Reflect on the past year: What were some of the goals you wanted to accomplish with your group? Who joined and what have they added to the group? What have you learned from everyone and from yourself? What will you take from this year and how will you use what you have learned going forward?

WRITE THEM OUT HERE:

Chapter 14

ENCOURAGED

This month focus on things that encourage you and your group.

GOD

Family & Friends

GOOD VIBES

#GOALS

Vision

CHAPTER 14

ENCOURAGED

Set a goal to spend the month focusing on being encouraged. This is an activity that the group can work on individually. It can be given out during a webinar or workshop, be a take home activity after another event, or be used in a retreat setting.

- ○ Encourage = to inspire with courage, spirit, or hope. (Merriam-Webster.com)

- ○ What is it that makes you feel encouraged?

- ○ What can you do on a daily basis to cultivate feelings of encouragement?

- ○ Our inner thoughts have a huge impact on our daily actions, energy levels, and can even affect our motivation to follow our goals. If needed, take a few minutes to write out or journal your thoughts.

- ○ Make a list of things that encourage you. If this is done in a group setting, you can have a discussion afterwards. Your list can include whatever makes you tick.

HERE ARE A FEW IDEAS TO GET YOU STARTED:

- ► Spending time with family or friends.
- ► Setting goals with the dates you want to accomplish them by.
- ► Making the decision that you will not let outside influences bring your spirits down.
- ► Spending time with God.

- ► Reading motivational quotes, blogs, or stories online.
- ► Reviewing your vision board daily, weekly, and monthly, revising as needed.
- ► Posting inspirational quotes & affirmations on social media, your bathroom mirror, or on your computer screen where you can see them daily.
- ► Taking daily steps to put your goals into action.
- ► Encouraging others.

○ Remember that you have the responsibility to design the life you want. Only you can make the choice to follow your dreams, to go after that which lifts your spirit, and live an encouraged life.

○ If you are doing this activity virtually, you can use an online site that everyone can log in to, and create a virtual word cloud as they enter words that represent things that encourage them.

○ Encourage the group to schedule some of their items in their planners to do throughout the year or add to their vision boards as a visual reminder of things that encourage them and keep them motivated.

SPOTLIGHT

Some days we can feel pressure from our day-to-day lives. Get this done, go here, do this for this person, go pick up this. It is easy and sometimes tempting to just get caught up in the mix. Self-care is so important to our wellbeing, mental health, overall health, and peace of mind. Take a few minutes to reflect back on the positive, the good things that have happened, encouraging words given or spoken, and goals accomplished. Once you have these, think of ways to stay encouraged.

"Life is short, and it's up to you to make it sweet."

Sadie Delany

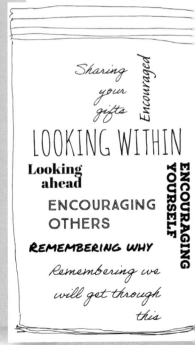

RUN ON – BY JAMILA KAMARIA BROWN

I could see myself dancing in the wind,

twirling to the rhythms and beats of the music.

I could feel the pulse of the percussion section,

vibrating in my joints and limbs.

I could imagine how I could touch someone's life through my dancing,

show them a piece of my world through my actions.

Let them bear witness to my dreams, the ones that lay down inside

invisible to the human eye.

Be encouraged, my sisters, to live on, press on, dream on.

Follow your dreams, and encourage others to follow theirs.

Live that abundant life! Unapologetically…

Take care of your heart, and continue to grow.

Don't allow the negativity and lies of others to define who you are.

Never forget that God doesn't make junk.

You are strong, you are beautiful, you are unique, you are awesome,

and only you can do you!

Remember the legacies of those who came before you,

but also create and live your own.

We all have something to give; we all have a purpose to fulfill.

Find yours, my sister, and run on.

Reviewing your vision board daily, weekly, and monthly, revising as needed

Spending time with family or friends

Reading motivational quotes, blogs, or stories online

Encouraging others

assure
inspire
motivate
uplift
ch
promote
positive

Setting goals with the dates you want to accomplish them by

Spending time with God

FOLLOW THE DREAMS OF YOUR HEART. YOU HAVE A PURPOSE THAT ONLY YOU CAN FULFILL. YOU HAVE A DREAM TO SHARE THAT ONLY YOU CAN SHARE.
– JAMILA K. BROWN

APPENDIX A: DISCONNECTED & DETACHED

CHILL TIME ACTIVITY FOR WOMEN'S RETREAT

Life happens, but what do you do when you are going through tough times? How do you smile and find the strength to go on when no one knows the battles you have faced and may still be facing? How do you encourage yourself so that you can encourage others? This is an opportunity for some quiet time. Encourage everyone to use the journaling sheets included in their packets to study the scriptures listed below. Meet back up as a group and discuss some ways to stay anchored and afloat.

SCRIPTURES:

- ○ John 17:20
- ○ Exodus 33:14
- ○ Joshua 1:9
- ○ Psalm 23:4
- ○ Matthew 28:20
- ○ Romans 8:38-39
- ○ Philippians 4:6-7
- ○ John 14:27
- ○ Nahum 1:7
- ○ Exodus 14:14
- ○ Psalm 4:8

STUDY QUESTIONS:

1. What are some ways you have dealt with life's issues in the past?

2. What are two things you can take away from the study scriptures to help you when you are going through?

3. Do you have another favorite scripture that you use to encourage yourself? If so write it out in your journal.

4. God's love for us is so amazing! Nothing that we go through, nothing said to us or about us, nothing withheld from us can separate us from his love. Nothing can ever change that fact! What are some ways God shows His love for us in the study scriptures?

5. It is easy to forget, that God is just a prayer away. Never underestimate the power of prayer. Write out a short prayer regarding your situation in your retreat journal.

6. What do the scriptures tell us about prayer and how can you apply it to your life?

7. What are some ways to take care of not just your physical wellbeing but your spiritual and mental wellbeing?

CLOSING PRAYER:

Thank you Father, for your reminder that you can use everything for my good. Even the things I have cried about, the things I have feared, my hopes, my doubts, my regrets, everything. You haven't forgotten me; I am most precious to You. You know my heart, its longings, its hopes, its truths. You have always known me. Thank you that even in this storm you see me and you know how my story will end. Thank you for restoring my sight, my focus, back onto what I should be doing – Being your light in the darkness of this world. Thank you for your love, for it is all that has sustained me. I pray these things in the name of your Son Jesus, Amen.

APPENDIX B: NOT WITHOUT HOPE

CHILL TIME ACTIVITY FOR WOMEN'S RETREAT

Because of all God has done for us, we do not live as if we have no hope. Our hope is in Him! Regardless of the things life brings our way, regardless of smiling when you would rather cry, in spite of the pain in the midst of a storm of life, reflect on the fact that God walks with us through it all. We must trust that He has our tomorrow and whatever it will bring. Have courage in knowing how well God knows and loves us.

SCRIPTURES

"This hope we have as an anchor of the soul, both sure and steadfast, and which enters the Presence behind the veil."

Hebrews 6:19 NKJV

"For I know the thoughts that I think towards you, says the Lord, thoughts of peace and not evil, to give you a future and a hope."

Jeremiah 29:11

REVIEW THE FOLLOWING STORIES IN GROUPS AND MEET BACK TO DISCUSS QUESTIONS AS AN OVERALL GROUP:

○ Ruth and Naomi - Ruth 1:1-5, 13-17, 2:11-23, 4:13-15

○ Hannah - 1 Samuel 1:1-2:11; 2:19-21

STUDY QUESTIONS:

1. List the situation of the woman in each story.

2. In the midst of what each woman was facing, what did she do?

3. How did each woman's story end?

4. How do you see hope reflected in each story?

5. What can you learn from each woman's life?

6. How does each woman's story teach us to be hopeful despite what we face in our lives?

7. What was a defining moment in the life of each woman that marked a change, growth, or gave you a glimpse of how God was moving in the midst of her life?

8. What is a defining moment in your own life that has marked a change or a turning point where you knew that what you had gone through was the beginning of something greater or was leading to something greater?

CLOSING PRAYER:

Thank you Father for hope today. Please replace my fears with the truth found in your word. I thank you in advance. Help me to have courage in knowing that you hear all of our prayers. The simple prayer, the extravagant prayer, the whispered prayer on our way out of the door. You hear them all. The number of words doesn't matter because you look at the heart. Remind me today that I do not need to fear because You are ultimately in control of all things, and you have promised never to leave me or forsake me. You have known all the days of my life before I was even born. Thank you for keeping me and for watching over me. Thank you for your promises, they bring me peace. I pray these things in the name of your Son Jesus, Amen.

APPENDIX C: COLORING SHEETS

DREAM CHASER

LIFE TO THE FULLEST

And the beautiful thing about God is this: even though we cannot fully comprehend His love, His love fully comprehends us.
—Morgan Harper Nichols

APPENDIX D:

MY GIFTS & PASSIONS POSTCARD TEMPLATE FOR "INSPIRE ME" VISION & GOALS POP-UP

YOUR GIFTS &
PASSIONS

THE GIFTS GOD HAS GIVEN ME:

I HAVE A PASSION FOR:

I CAN USE MY GIFTS EVERYDAY TO:

JAMILA BROWN RESIDES IN NORTHERN CALIFORNIA. SHE IS AN OUTREACH COORDINATOR, GARDENER, COOKIE BAKER, LOVER OF TACOS, AMATEUR PHOTOGRAPHER, ENCOURAGER, SINGER, POET, CURLY GIRL, GOAL SETTING, LOVER OF LIFE, AND A WOMAN THANKFUL FOR GOD'S LOVE AND GRACE. SHE HAS A BACHELOR OF SCIENCE IN BUSINESS ADMINISTRATION MANAGEMENT AND A MASTER OF BUSINESS ADMINISTRATION. JAMILA HAS PLANNED MANY DIFFERENT TYPES OF EVENTS FROM BABY SHOWERS TO WOMEN'S RETREATS, TO FINANCIAL AID WORKSHOPS AND CHOCOLATE PARTIES. SHE ENJOYS THE COLLABORATION AND CREATIVE OUTLET, PUTTING ALL THE PIECES TOGETHER TO SEE EVENTS COME OFF WELL, AND OFFERING OPPORTUNITIES TO REACH WOMEN OF ALL AGES TO ENCOURAGE THEM TO UNWIND AND HAVE SOME FUN. WE GET ONE LIFE TO LIVE, LET'S MAKE IT AN ENJOYABLE ONE!

JAMILA BROWN

SARAH GRIFFITH

SARAH GRIFFITH WAS NATIVE TO CALIFORNIA AND WAS BORN IN SAN FRANCISCO. SARAH WAS INTERESTED IN ARTS AND CRAFTS FROM AN EARLY AGE. HER MOTHER WAS AN ARTIST AND SEAMSTRESS WHO WOULD BUY HER NUMBERED ART PICTURES TO DO. SHE ALSO ENJOYED MAKING CLOTHING FOR HER BARBIE DOLLS. IN ELEMENTARY SCHOOL, SHE LEARNED TO CROCHET AND KNIT. WHEN SHE GOT OLDER, SHE KNEW SHE WANTED TO GO TO AN ART SCHOOL. SHE STARTED DRAWING PORTRAITS OF STUDENTS AND MAKING CROCHET HATS IN JUNIOR COLLEGE. SHE NEXT APPLIED TO ART SCHOOL AND WAS ACCEPTED INTO THE CALIFORNIA COLLEGE OF ARTS AND CRAFTS IN OAKLAND, CALIFORNIA. THERE SHE DEVELOPED HER SKILLS FOR DRAWING, PAINTING, CERAMICS, AND ART APPRECIATION. SHE USED HER ART SKILLS WITH CHILDREN IN THE CLASSROOM FOR OVER THIRTY YEARS. HER LOVE AND DEDICATION WILL REMAIN WITH US FOREVER.

AFIYA GRIFFITH

AFIYA GRIFFITH IS CURRENTLY A CHEF LIVING IN MIAMI FLORIDA, ORIGINALLY BORN AND RAISED IN CALIFORNIA WITH HER FAMILY OF 7. FOOD HAS ALWAYS BEEN SOMETHING THAT SHE'S BEEN OVERZEALOUS ABOUT, BEFORE SHE COULD REMEMBER HER PASSION FOR BEAUTIFUL AND TASTY FOOD, HAS ALWAYS DRIVEN HER TO PREPARING AND SHOPPING FOR FOOD FOR HER FAMILY AND FRIENDS. AFIYA STUDIED CULINARY ARTS AT THE WELL KNOWN JOHNSON & WALES UNIVERSITY, WHERE SHE OBTAINED HER ASSOCIATE IN SCIENCE IN CULINARY ARTS AND BACHELOR OF SCIENCE IN FOOD SERVICE MANAGEMENT. COMBINING HER PASSION FOR FOOD AND SERVICE, AFIYA HAS BEEN FORTUNATE TO WORK FOR GREAT COMPANIES AND RESTAURANTS SUCH AS "MARKET" BY ACCLAIMED CHEF JEAN GEORGE AND PRINCESS CRUISES. HER DRIVE AND DREAMS TO BRING DELICIOUS FOOD TO EVERYONE HAS MOTIVATED HER TO BE THE BEST CHEF THAT SHE KNOWS TO BE AND ALL WHO HAVE HAD THE OPPORTUNITY TO ENJOY HER FOOD CAN KINDLY AGREE.

WE ALL HAVE SOMETHING TO GIVE;
WE ALL HAVE A PURPOSE TO FULFILL.
FIND YOURS MY SISTER AND RUN ON.
JAMILA K. BROWN

Made in the USA
Monee, IL
07 January 2025

b8af921e-d50d-449a-9586-964d6259c352R01